GORDON RAMSAY'S
Greatest Hits

RECIPES FROM THE f WORD

Food by
Gordon Ramsay
with Mark Sargeant

Text by
Emily Quah

Photographs by
Lisa Barber & Jill Mead

Quadrille
PUBLISHING

notes

All spoon measures are level unless otherwise stated:
1 tsp = 5ml spoon; 1 tbsp = 15ml spoon.

All herbs are fresh, and all pepper is freshly ground unless
otherwise suggested.

I recommend using free-range eggs. If you are pregnant or in
a vulnerable health group, avoid those recipes that contain
raw egg whites or lightly cooked eggs.

If possible, buy unwaxed citrus fruit if you are using the zest.

My oven timings are for fan-assisted ovens. If you are using
a conventional oven, increase the temperature by 10–15°C
(1 Gas Mark). Individual ovens can deviate by as much as
10°C from the setting, either way. Get to know your oven and
use an oven thermometer to check its accuracy. My cooking
times are provided as guidelines, with a description of colour
or texture where appropriate.

contents

breakfast & brunch

Melon & berry salad

Serves 4

1 canteloupe melon
1 honeydew melon
300g mixed berries, such as blueberries,
    blackberries and raspberries
1 lime
1 orange
1–2 tsp runny honey, to drizzle
handful of mint, shredded

Halve the melons, remove and discard the seeds, then use a melon baller to carve out the flesh in balls (or simply cut it into small chunks if you prefer).

Divide the melon balls and mixed berries between individual serving bowls (or simply toss them together in a large salad bowl).

Finely grate the zests from the lime and orange over the fruit salad. Cut the lime and orange in half and squeeze a little juice over each serving. Drizzle with a little honey, then scatter over the shredded mint.

Best served slightly chilled.

Lightly spiced dried fruit compote

Serves 4–5

150g dried prunes
150g dried apricots
100g dried cherries or cranberries
100g dried blueberries
1 cinnamon stick
2 star anise
finely grated zest of 1 large orange
juice of 2 large oranges
100ml water
2 tbsp Grand Marnier (optional)
low-fat natural or Greek yoghurt, to serve

Put all the dried fruit in a small saucepan with the spices, orange zest and juice, water and liqueur, if using. Give the mixture a stir and slowly bring to the boil. Reduce the heat to low and cover the pan with a lid.

Simmer the mixture, giving it an occasional stir, for about 8–10 minutes until the fruit is soft and plump and the liquid has reduced and is syrupy. You may need to add a splash of water towards the end if the mixture looks too dry.

Tip into a bowl and leave to cool slightly. Serve in individual bowls topped with a spoonful of yoghurt.

Granola with dried cranberries

Serves 4–5

250g jumbo rolled oats
50g nibbed or flaked almonds
50g pumpkin seeds
50g sunflower seeds
1 tsp ground ginger
pinch of salt
50g butter
5–6 tbsp honey
finely grated zest of 1 large orange
100g dried cranberries or
   blueberries

Heat the oven to 180°C/Gas 4. In a large bowl, mix together the oats, almonds, pumpkin seeds, sunflower seeds, ground ginger and salt. Melt the butter with the honey, then add the grated orange zest. Pour over the oat mixture and stir well.

Spread the mixture on a wide baking tray and bake for 15–20 minutes until golden brown, giving it a stir every 5 minutes to ensure it colours evenly. Allow to cool and crisp up, then stir in the dried fruit. Store in an airtight container until ready to eat.

Porridge

Serves 4

150g porridge oats or medium ground
  oatmeal
500ml water
500ml semi-skimmed milk
pinch of fine sea salt (optional)

To serve
4 tbsp low-fat natural or Greek yoghurt
runny honey or brown sugar
handful of toasted flaked almonds

Put the oats, water, milk and salt, if using, into a medium saucepan. Stir well, then place over a high heat until the mixture is almost boiling. Turn the heat down to low and stir frequently for 5–8 minutes as the porridge bubbles and thickens. Continue to cook until it is the consistency you like, adding a splash of water if you prefer a thinner porridge.

Take the pan from the heat and divide the porridge between warm bowls. Top each portion with a spoonful of yoghurt, a little honey or brown sugar and a scattering of toasted almonds.

Also delicious eaten with fresh fruit in season, or dried fruit compote (see page 11).

Full english breakfast
Serves 4

olive oil, to brush and drizzle
4 portabello mushrooms, cleaned
300g vine-ripened cherry tomatoes
sea salt and black pepper
16 rashers of smoked back bacon
8 large eggs
dash of white wine vinegar
8 slices of rye bread, toasted

Preheat the grill to the highest setting. Half-fill a wide, shallow pan with water and bring to a simmer. Line a large (or two small) baking sheet(s) with foil, then brush over with a little olive oil.

Trim the mushrooms, removing their stalks, then lay, cap side down, on the baking sheet. Place the vine tomatoes alongside. Drizzle over a little olive oil and sprinkle with a pinch each of salt and pepper. Lay the bacon rashers in a single layer on the baking sheet (the second one if using two). Place under the grill for 5 minutes until the mushrooms are tender and the bacon is golden brown around the edges.

To poach the eggs, break each one into a cup or ramekin. Add a dash of vinegar to the pan of simmering water. Whisk the water in a circular motion to create a whirlpool effect. Gently slide the eggs into the centre of the whirlpool, one at a time, then reduce the heat to a low simmer. Poach for 1½ minutes if the eggs were at room temperature, or 2 minutes if they were straight from the fridge. The whites will have set but the yolks should still be runny in the middle.

Divide the bacon, mushrooms, tomatoes and rye toasts between warm serving plates. Carefully lift out each poached egg with a slotted spoon, dab the bottom of the spoon with kitchen paper to absorb any excess water and slide onto a rye toast. Grind some pepper over the eggs and serve at once.

Buckwheat pancakes with smoked salmon

Serves 5–6

85g buckwheat flour
85g plain flour
1½ tsp baking powder
⅓ tsp fine sea salt
1 tbsp caster sugar
200ml semi-skimmed milk
1½ tsp melted butter or light olive oil
2 large egg whites
small knob of butter

To serve
10–12 slices of smoked salmon
6 tbsp soured cream
3–4 tbsp capers, rinsed and drained
handful of salad leaves (optional)
olive oil, to drizzle (optional)
black pepper

Mix the flours, baking powder, salt and sugar together in a large mixing bowl. Make a well in the centre and add the milk and melted butter or oil. Gradually draw the flour mix into the centre, stirring to combine the ingredients to make a smooth batter. Leave to stand for a few minutes.

When ready to cook, whisk the egg whites in a clean bowl to firm peaks, then fold into the pancake batter. Melt a small knob of butter in each of two non-stick blini pans or one large non-stick frying pan, to lightly coat the base.

Add a small ladleful of batter to each blini pan (or two to the frying pan) and cook over a medium heat for 1½–2 minutes until golden brown on the underside. Flip the pancakes over and cook on the other side for another minute. Slide onto a warm plate and keep warm, while you cook the rest of the batter to make 10–12 pancakes in total. After the first pancake, you probably won't need to add extra butter to the pans.

Divide the pancakes between warm serving plates and drape a couple of smoked salmon slices around. Drop a spoonful of soured cream in the middle and scatter over the capers and salad leaves, if using. Drizzle with a little olive oil and grind over some black pepper.

Scrambled eggs with anchovy & asparagus

Serves 4

350g asparagus spears
sea salt and black pepper
100g marinated anchovy fillets
   (available in tubs from delis and good
   supermarkets)
10 large free-range eggs
knob of butter
4 large basil leaves, roughly chopped
a little olive oil, to drizzle (optional)

To prepare the asparagus, snap off the woody
base of the stalks. Bring a pan of salted water to the boil and blanch
the asparagus spears for 3–4 minutes or until tender. Meanwhile, chop
2 anchovies very finely.

Break the eggs into a cold, heavy-based pan and add a
knob of butter and the chopped anchovies. Place the pan on the lowest
heat possible and, using a heatproof spatula, stir the eggs vigorously
to begin with to combine the yolks with the whites, then intermittently
but frequently.

As the eggs begin to set, add a little salt,
some pepper and the chopped basil to the mixture. They will take about
4 minutes to scramble and you might need to keep moving the pan on
and off the heat so that they don't get overheated. The scrambled eggs
should still be soft and creamy.

Drain the asparagus as soon as it is ready and dab
dry with kitchen paper. Divide between warm serving plates. Pile the
hot scrambled eggs on top and drape a couple of anchovy fillets over
each serving. If you wish, drizzle a little olive oil around the plate.
Serve immediately.

Herb omelette with cherry tomatoes

Serves 1

8–10 cherry tomatoes
1 tbsp olive oil
sea salt and black pepper
3 large eggs
handful of mixed herbs, such as flat leaf
    parsley, chives and chervil, chopped

Halve the cherry tomatoes or cut into
quarters and place in a bowl. Heat the olive oil in a non-stick omelette pan and tip in the tomatoes. Season with salt and pepper and fry over a medium heat for 1–2 minutes until the tomatoes are just soft but still retaining their shape.

Lightly beat the eggs in a bowl in the meantime.
Scatter the chopped herbs over the tomatoes, then pour in the beaten eggs. Quickly stir and shake the pan to distribute the eggs and ensure they cook evenly. When they are almost set, take the pan off the heat.

Fold the omelette, using a heatproof spatula to lift
one edge and tipping the pan slightly to make it easier to fold over. Slide onto a warm plate and serve immediately.

Berry & yoghurt smoothie

Serves 4–6

200g raspberries
200g blackberries
6 heaped tbsp natural yoghurt
300ml milk
3–4 tbsp icing sugar or maple syrup,
   to taste

Place all the ingredients in a blender and whiz until smooth, sweetening the mixture with icing sugar or maple syrup to taste. Serve in chilled glasses.

more ideas for smoothies...

Fig, honey and yoghurt Trim 8 ripe figs, removing the tops, then cut into quarters. Put into a blender along with 600ml semi-skimmed milk, 200ml natural yoghurt and 6–8 tbsp honey to taste. Add 4–6 ice cubes, for extra chill if you like. Blend until smooth and thick, then pour into chilled glasses. Serves 4

Pomegranate and banana Peel 3 large ripe bananas, cut into chunks and freeze in a plastic bag for an hour. Drop the banana chunks into a blender. Scrape the seeds from a vanilla pod with the back of a knife and add them to the blender. Pour in 250ml pomegranate juice, 500ml natural yoghurt and 1–2 tbsp honey. Blend until smooth and serve in chilled glasses. Serves 4

Wholemeal blueberry muffins

Makes 12

2 very ripe large bananas
300g wholemeal flour
1½ tsp baking powder
1 tsp bicarbonate of soda
pinch of fine sea salt
100g light muscovado or brown sugar
284ml carton buttermilk
1 large egg, lightly beaten
75g light olive oil (or melted butter)
200g blueberries, rinsed and drained
1 tbsp demerara sugar

Heat the oven to 180°C/Gas 4. Line a 12-hole muffin tin with muffin cases. Peel the bananas and mash in a bowl, using a fork.

Mix the flour, baking powder, bicarbonate of soda, salt and brown sugar together in a large mixing bowl. Make a well in the centre and add the buttermilk, egg, olive oil and bananas. Quickly fold the ingredients together until just incorporated, taking care not to overmix. Tip in the blueberries and give the batter one or two stirs.

Spoon the batter into the muffin cases and sprinkle with the demerara sugar. The cases will be quite full. Bake in the oven for about 20–25 minutes until well risen and golden brown on top; a skewer inserted into the centre of the muffin should emerge clean.

Leave to cool in the tin for a couple of minutes, then transfer to a wire rack to cool completely.

Date, walnut & linseed bread

Makes one 900g loaf

50g unsalted butter, diced, plus extra
   to grease

250g medjool dates, pitted and chopped

2 tbsp (about 30–40g) molasses

250ml water

250g plain flour

250g wholemeal flour

½ tsp fine sea salt

125g light muscovado or brown sugar

2 tsp baking powder

2 large eggs, lightly beaten

1 tsp vanilla extract

50g chopped walnuts

30g linseed

Heat the oven to 170°C/Gas 3. Butter a 900g loaf tin, preferably non-stick. Put the butter, chopped dates, molasses and water in a small pan over a low heat. Stir until the butter and molasses have melted, then take off the heat and leave to cool.

Put the flours, salt, sugar and baking powder into a large mixing bowl and stir to combine. Make a well in the centre. Add the eggs and vanilla extract, then pour the date mixture into the well. Fold through the ingredients until evenly incorporated, but don't overmix. Finally, fold through the chopped walnuts and linseed.

Spoon the mixture into the prepared tin and spread evenly. Bake for about 1 hour until a skewer inserted into the centre of the loaf comes out clean. Turn out onto a wire rack and leave to cool completely before slicing.

Delicious served just as it is, or lightly toasted with cheese.

Seeded honey loaf

Makes two 500g loaves

15g fresh yeast (or 7g sachet fast-action
    dried yeast)
275ml tepid water
225g wholemeal flour
225g strong white flour, plus extra to dust
1½ tsp fine sea salt
50g mixed seeds (about 2 tsp each of
    poppy, sesame, pumpkin, linseed and
    sunflower)
3 tbsp olive oil, plus extra to oil
2 tbsp honey
2 tbsp milk, to glaze

If using fresh yeast, put 3–4 tbsp of the water into a warm bowl, crumble in the yeast and stir to dissolve. Leave to sponge for a few minutes.

Put the flours and salt into a large mixing bowl, add the seeds and stir to mix. (If you're using fast-action dried yeast, stir this into the flour mixture.) Make a well in the centre and add the olive oil, honey, yeast mixture and remaining water (all of it if using dried yeast). Stir with a wooden spoon to combine, adding more flour if the dough seems too wet. It should be soft, but not sticky.

Press the dough into a ball, then knead on a lightly floured surface for about 5–10 minutes until smooth. Place in a lightly oiled bowl, cover with lightly oiled cling film and leave the dough to rise in a warm part of the kitchen for an hour or so until doubled in size.

Punch the dough down on a lightly floured surface and knead it lightly. Divide into two pieces and shape each one into a round loaf. Place each on a lightly oiled large baking sheet and cover with lightly oiled cling film. Leave to prove in a warm spot until almost doubled in size.

Heat the oven to 200°C/Gas 6. Remove the cling film and brush a thin layer of milk over the loaves. Bake for about 20–25 minutes until light golden in colour. The loaves should sound hollow when tapped underside. Leave to cool on a wire rack. Best served slightly warm.

Bircher muesli

Serves 4

200g rolled oats
about 400ml semi-skimmed milk
1 apple
1 tbsp runny honey, plus extra to
   drizzle
150ml low-fat natural yoghurt
splash of apple juice

To serve
fresh berries
toasted walnuts

Put the oats into a bowl and pour on the milk. Cover and refrigerate for at least an hour, ideally overnight.

Coarsely grate the apple over the oats, discarding the core and pips. Stir in the honey and yoghurt, then add a splash of apple juice or a little more milk to loosen the mixture if it is too thick.

Serve each portion of muesli drizzled with a little more honey and topped with fresh berries and toasted walnuts.

Banana oat muffins

Makes 12

100g oats
200g plain flour
1½ tsp baking powder
1 tsp bicarbonate of soda
¼ tsp sea salt
100g light brown sugar
4 large ripe bananas
1 large egg, beaten
60g butter, melted or light olive oil
75g walnuts, chopped

Heat the oven to 180°C/Gas 4. Line a 12-hole muffin tin with paper cases. In a large bowl, mix the oats, flour, baking powder, bicarbonate of soda, salt and sugar. Make a well in the centre.

Mash the bananas in another bowl with a fork. Stir in the beaten egg and melted butter or olive oil. Add to the dry mixture with the chopped walnuts and fold through until just combined (don't overmix). Spoon into the paper cases and bake for 20–25 minutes until brown and a skewer inserted in the middle comes out clean. Leave in the tin for a few minutes, then transfer to a wire rack. Best served warm.

Cranachan with blackberries

Serves 4

4 tbsp medium ground porridge oats
200g blackberries, plus extra to serve
about 5 tbsp runny honey
300ml fromage frais
300ml crème fraîche
1–2 tbsp whisky

Lightly toast the oats in a dry pan, tossing frequently for 2–3 minutes until lightly golden. Tip onto a plate and leave to cool.

Purée the berries with the honey in a blender or food processor. Tip into a large bowl and add the fromage frais, crème fraîche, whisky and all but 1 tbsp of the toasted oats. Stir lightly to create a rippled effect. Spoon into glasses, top with a few blackberries and sprinkle with the toasted oatmeal.

Oaty walnut & cheese scones

Makes 10–12

350g self-raising flour, plus extra to dust
1 tsp fine sea salt
2 tsp baking powder
pinch of cayenne pepper
60g butter, diced
150g rolled oats, plus extra to sprinkle
100g mature Cheddar cheese, grated
100g walnuts, chopped
2 large eggs, beaten
9 tbsp buttermilk, plus milk to brush

Heat the oven to 180°C/Gas 4. Sift the flour, salt, baking powder and cayenne into a large bowl. Add the butter and rub in until the mixture resembles fine crumbs. Stir in the oats, cheese and nuts. Make a well in the centre, add the eggs and buttermilk and mix until the dough comes together, adding a little more buttermilk if needed.

Gently roll out on a lightly floured surface to a 2.5cm thickness and stamp out rounds with a 6cm cutter. Place, slightly apart, on a baking sheet, then brush the tops with milk and sprinkle with 1 tbsp oats. Bake for 15–20 minutes until golden brown. Serve warm.

snacks

Pata negra, melon & mozzarella focaccia

Serves 4

4 large pieces of focaccia
(about 8 x 10cm)

4 thin slices of ripe cantaloupe or
charantais melon

8 slices of fresh buffalo mozzarella

4 or 8 slices of pata negra ham

few basil leaves

extra virgin olive oil, to drizzle

sea salt and black pepper

Split the focaccia in half. Place the bottom halves on plates and top with the melon slices.

Drape the mozzarella and ham slices on top of the melon and scatter over a few basil leaves.

Drizzle lightly with extra virgin olive oil, sprinkle with a little sea salt and grind over some black pepper. Sandwich together with the top focaccia halves and serve.

Pan-roasted vegetable panini

Serves 4

2–3 tbsp olive oil

1 red onion, peeled and chopped

few thyme sprigs

1 courgette, chopped

1 red pepper, deseeded and chopped

1 yellow pepper, deseeded and chopped

sea salt and black pepper

4 panini buns

pesto, for spreading

pecorino shavings, to sprinkle

small handful of pine nuts, toasted

Heat the olive oil in a wide frying pan. Fry the onion with the thyme sprigs over a high heat for 3–4 minutes until it begins to soften. Tip in the chopped courgette and peppers and cook for a few minutes, stirring often, until the vegetables are just tender. Season with salt and pepper to taste. Discard the thyme sprigs.

Split the panini buns in half and spread both halves with pesto. Divide the vegetables among the bases and scatter over some shaved pecorino and the pine nuts. Sandwich together with the panini tops.

Grill each sandwich in a panini press or toasted sandwich maker for a few minutes until compressed and warmed through.

Fresh tuna open sandwich

Serves 4

2 thick tuna steaks
sea salt and black pepper
olive oil, to cook and drizzle
1–2 baby cos lettuce, trimmed
balsamic vinegar, to drizzle
4 thick slices of crusty white bread
4 tbsp tapenade or pesto

Season the tuna steaks on both sides with salt and pepper and quickly sear in a very hot pan with a little olive oil, allowing 1½–2 minutes each side. Cool slightly.

Separate the lettuce leaves and toss in a bowl with a drizzle of olive oil and balsamic vinegar.

Toast the bread and spread each slice with 1 tbsp tapenade or pesto. Lay on plates and pile the lettuce leaves on top. Thickly slice the tuna steaks and arrange over the lettuce. Sprinkle with a little salt, black pepper and olive oil, then serve.

Smoked salmon & cream cheese on rye
Serves 4

200g cream cheese
½ tsp cracked black pepper
pinch of sea salt
8 slices of rye bread
2–3 slices of smoked salmon
oscietra caviar (optional)

Season the cream cheese with the cracked pepper and salt. Spread thickly onto the slices of rye bread. (Keep any remaining peppered cream cheese in the fridge for another sandwich.)

Lay the slices of smoked salmon on half of the bread slices, then top with a generous spoonful of oscietra caviar for a touch of luxury, if you like. Sandwich together with the rest of the bread slices and serve.

Devilled caesar salad

Serves 4

8 slices of Parma ham
tiny drizzle of olive oil
8 thick slices of ciabatta
4 baby gem lettuce, trimmed and washed
15–16 (about 60g) marinated fresh
   anchovy fillets
Parmesan shavings, to finish

Dressing
1 garlic clove, peeled and crushed
2 salted anchovies, rinsed, drained and
   finely chopped
½ tsp paprika
few dashes of Worcestershire sauce
100g low-fat natural or Greek yoghurt
black pepper

To make the dressing, whiz all the ingredients together in a food processor, seasoning with pepper to taste. You will probably find that the anchovies provide enough salt.

Cook the Parma ham in two batches. Heat a tiny drizzle of olive oil in a non-stick frying pan and lay half of the ham slices in the pan. Fry over a medium heat for a couple of minutes on each side until golden brown, then transfer to a plate. Cook the rest in the same way. Leave until cool and crisp, then break the Parma ham slices into smaller pieces.

Lightly toast the ciabatta slices in the same pan, turning to colour both sides. Remove and cut into chunky croûtons. Separate the lettuce leaves and divide between serving plates. Scatter over the croûtons, Parma ham and anchovies. Drizzle over the dressing and top with Parmesan shavings to serve.

Pastrami & cream cheese bagel
Serves 2

2 poppyseed bagels
100g cream cheese
1 tbsp wholegrain mustard
sea salt and black pepper
4–6 slices of pastrami
2 large gherkins, sliced
large handful of rocket leaves

Split the bagels in half and lightly toast them until golden on both sides.

Mix the cream cheese with the mustard and salt and pepper to taste. Spread evenly on the bagel halves.

Arrange 2 or 3 pastrami slices, a sliced gherkin and a small handful of rocket leaves on each bagel base. Sandwich together with the bagel tops.

Poached duck egg with anchovy fingers

Serves 4

4 very fresh duck eggs, at room temperature
1 tsp white wine vinegar

Anchovy fingers
2 tbsp tapenade
4 slices of medium sliced white bread
about 16 salted anchovies in oil, drained
3–4 tbsp olive oil

To be ready to poach the eggs, bring a wide, deep saucepan of water to a simmer and add the vinegar.

For the anchovy fingers, spread the tapenade on 2 slices of white bread and arrange the anchovies on top. Cover with the remaining bread slices, then flatten the sandwiches with a rolling pin and cut off the crusts. Heat the olive oil in a frying pan and fry the anchovy sandwiches until golden brown on both sides. Remove and drain on kitchen paper, then slice into 1cm wide fingers; keep warm.

Crack the duck eggs, one at a time, into a teacup and slide them into the slowly simmering water. Poach for 2–3 minutes until the whites are set and the yolks are still runny in the middle. With a slotted spoon, carefully remove each one and place in a warm small bowl. Serve with the anchovy fingers, for dipping into the runny yolk.

Crayfish, avocado & mayo toasties

Serves 4

400g cooked crayfish tails
4–5 tbsp mayonnaise
½ tsp white truffle-infused olive oil
1 avocado, chopped
sea salt and black pepper
4 thick slices of rustic white bread

Toss the cooked crayfish tails with the mayonnaise and olive oil. Stir through the avocado and season with sea salt and black pepper to taste.

Lightly toast the bread slices. Sandwich the crayfish filling between the toast slices and serve.

Scrambled eggs with crabmeat & chives

Serves 4

30g butter
12 large eggs, lightly beaten
200g white (or mixture of white and
   brown) crabmeat, picked through
handful of chives, finely chopped
sea salt and black pepper
2 tbsp crème fraîche
4 thick slices of country bread, toasted

Melt the butter in a non-stick saucepan and add the beaten eggs. Stir with a wooden spoon over a low heat for a few minutes until the eggs are half-set but still quite runny.

Stir in the crabmeat, chives and seasoning. Keep stirring until the eggs are just about to set, then quickly incorporate the crème fraîche and remove the pan from the heat.

Place a slice of toast on each warm plate and spoon the scrambled eggs on top. Serve immediately.

Baked egg florentine

Serves 4

30g butter
450g spinach leaves, washed and dried
sea salt and black pepper
4 large eggs, at room temperature
6–8 tbsp crème fraîche
nutmeg, for grating

Heat the oven to 200°C/Gas 6. Melt the butter in a large pan over a high heat. Add the spinach leaves and some seasoning and stir for a few seconds until the spinach has just wilted.

Divide the spinach among 4 buttered individual ceramic baking dishes and spread evenly, making a slight indentation in the centre. Leave to cool slightly.

Crack an egg into each indentation, then carefully spoon the crème fraîche around. Season with a sprinkling of salt, pepper and freshly grated nutmeg.

Bake in the oven for 10–12 minutes until the egg whites are set, but the yolks are still quite soft and runny in the centre. Serve immediately.

Flatbread, feta & chickpea salad

Serves 3–4

2 large, thin flatbreads or pita breads
½ tsp paprika
4 tbsp olive oil
1 red onion, peeled and thinly sliced
2 garlic cloves, peeled and thinly sliced
½ red chilli, deseeded and finely
   chopped
400g can chickpeas, rinsed and drained
generous squeeze of lemon juice
large handful of flat leaf parsley leaves
sea salt and black pepper
150g feta cheese

Heat the oven to 180°C/Gas 4. Split the breads horizontally. Mix the paprika with 2 tbsp of the olive oil. Brush each piece of bread with this mixture and place on a baking sheet. Bake until lightly golden brown and crisp, just 2–3 minutes for thin flatbreads, 4–5 minutes for pita bread.

Meanwhile, heat the remaining olive oil in a pan, add the onion and cook, stirring, over a medium heat for 6–8 minutes until soft. Add the garlic and chilli and fry for another minute. Tip in the chickpeas and stir to mix. Squeeze over the lemon juice and add the parsley and a little seasoning to taste.

Warm the chickpeas through, then tip into a large bowl and leave to stand for a few minutes. Crumble over two-thirds of the cheese and toss well.

Divide between serving plates and crumble over the remaining feta. Break the bread into smaller pieces and serve on the side.

everyday

Persian-style onion soup

Serves 4

3 tbsp olive oil

5 large onions, peeled and thinly sliced

sea salt and black pepper

½ tsp ground turmeric

½ tsp fenugreek seeds

½ tsp dried mint

2 tbsp plain flour

700ml Vegetable stock (see page 249) or
    Chicken stock (see page 248)

1 cinnamon stick

juice of 1 lemon

1 tsp caster sugar

few flat leaf parsley sprigs, chopped

Place a heavy-based pan over a medium heat. Add 2 tbsp olive oil, the onions and some seasoning. Cover and sweat for 12–15 minutes until the onions are soft, lifting the lid and stirring occasionally. Remove the lid and increase the heat very slightly.

Add the spices, dried mint and remaining oil, then stir in the flour. Cook, stirring frequently, for 3–4 minutes. Gradually pour in the stock, whisking as you do so to prevent any lumps forming. When it has all been added, drop in the cinnamon stick and simmer over a low heat, partially covered with the lid, for 30–40 minutes.

Stir in the lemon juice and sugar, then taste and adjust the seasoning. Discard the cinnamon stick. Ladle the soup into warm bowls and scatter over the parsley to serve.

Borscht

Serves 4

2 tbsp olive oil

1 onion, peeled and finely chopped

2 celery sticks, trimmed and finely chopped

1 large carrot, peeled and finely chopped

1 thyme sprig, leaves stripped

sea salt and black pepper

500g raw beetroot, peeled and chopped

¼ red cabbage, about 250g, finely chopped

800ml Vegetable stock (see page 249) or water

1 tbsp red wine vinegar, to taste

1 tsp caster sugar, to taste

handful of dill, chopped

4 tbsp soured cream or natural yoghurt, to serve (optional)

Heat the olive oil in a large pan and add the onion, celery, carrot, thyme leaves and some seasoning. Cook over a medium heat, stirring frequently, for 8–10 minutes.

Add the beetroot and cabbage with a small splash of water. Stir well, then cover and cook for 10–12 minutes until the vegetables are just tender. Lift the lid and give the mixture a stir several times during cooking to stop the vegetables catching and burning on the bottom of the pan.

Remove the lid and pour in the stock or water to cover the vegetables. Add the wine vinegar, bring to the boil, then reduce the heat to a simmer. Cook for another 5–10 minutes until the vegetables are soft. Skim off any froth from the surface. Adjust the seasoning to taste with salt, pepper and sugar.

Purée the soup with a stick blender until smooth and creamy, or leave it chunky for a traditional, rustic finish. If you decide to purée the soup, you may need to thin it down slightly with a little boiling water.

Ladle into warm bowls if serving hot; otherwise allow to cool, then chill thoroughly. Serve topped with the chopped dill and a dollop of soured cream or yoghurt.

Leek, potato & smoked haddock soup

Serves 4

3 tbsp olive oil, plus extra to drizzle
2 large leeks, trimmed and thinly sliced
500g Charlotte potatoes, peeled and cut
   into 1cm cubes
1 tsp curry powder
sea salt and black pepper
400ml milk (whole or semi-skimmed)
300ml Fish stock (see page 248) or
   Vegetable stock (see page 249)
1 bay leaf
250g smoked haddock fillets
knob of butter
small bunch of chives, finely chopped

Heat the olive oil in a large pan and sauté the leeks, potatoes, curry powder and seasoning over medium heat for 5 minutes or until the leeks have softened. Add the milk, stock and bay leaf, bring to the boil, then simmer for 5 minutes until the potatoes are tender.

Add the fish and poach for 2–3 minutes until flaky. Lift out with a slotted spoon and break into large flakes, removing the skin. Transfer a quarter of the leeks and potatoes to a bowl, add the butter and crush lightly with a fork. Stir through the haddock and chives.

Discard the bay leaf and whiz the soup with a blender until smooth and creamy. Check the seasoning and reheat, adding a little extra hot stock or water to thin if needed. Pile the crushed potato and haddock mixture in the centre of warm bowls and pour the soup around. Drizzle with a little olive oil and serve.

Butter bean, chorizo & red onion soup

Serves 4

225g chorizo sausage, skin removed

3 tbsp olive oil, plus extra to drizzle

2 red onions, peeled and finely chopped

2 garlic cloves, peeled and very finely
sliced

few thyme sprigs

2 x 420g cans butter beans, drained and
rinsed

sea salt and black pepper

squeeze of lemon juice

large handful of flat leaf parsley,
roughly chopped

Chop the chorizo into small bite-sized pieces. Put the kettle on to boil.

Heat the olive oil in a heavy-based saucepan and add the onions, garlic and thyme. Cook, stirring, for 2 minutes then add the chorizo. Stir over a high heat for a few minutes until the oil has taken on a reddish-golden hue from the chorizo.

Tip in the butter beans and pour in just enough boiling water to cover them. Bring to a simmer and cook gently for about 10 minutes.

Season generously with salt and pepper and add a squeeze of lemon juice. Scatter over the chopped parsley and ladle the soup into warm bowls to serve.

Cod & tomato chowder

Serves 4–5

3 tbsp olive oil

2 medium onions, peeled and roughly
   chopped

2 celery sticks, trimmed and roughly
   chopped

sea salt and black pepper

2 large carrots, peeled and roughly
   chopped

2 large waxy potatoes, about 400g,
   peeled and roughly chopped

1 yellow pepper, cored, deseeded and
   roughly chopped

few thyme sprigs

1 bay leaf

400g can chopped tomatoes

900ml Fish or Chicken stock
   (see page 248)

150g green beans, cut into short lengths

2 courgettes, roughly chopped

few dashes of Tabasco sauce (optional)

600g cod fillets, skinned and pin-boned

bunch of flat leaf parsley, roughly
   chopped

Heat the olive oil in a heavy-based pan. Add the onions, celery and some salt and pepper, and cook, stirring, over a medium heat for 6–8 minutes to soften. Add the carrots, potatoes, yellow pepper and herbs, and sauté for 5 minutes until the vegetables are lightly golden.

Add the tomatoes to the pan and pour in the stock. Cover and simmer for about 7–9 minutes until the vegetables are tender. Now tip in the green beans and courgettes, give the mixture a stir and simmer for another 3 minutes. Check the seasoning, adding a few dashes of Tabasco to spice up the chowder if you like.

Lightly season the cod fillets and lay them on top of the vegetables in the pan. Cover the pan again and simmer for 3–4 minutes until the fish is opaque and just cooked through.

Using a spoon, gently break the fish into large flakes. Ladle the hot soup into warm bowls and scatter a handful of chopped parsley over each serving.

Soba noodle soup with chicken & shiitake

Serves 4

2 large boneless, skinless chicken
  breasts, about 150g each
1 tbsp tamari or light soy sauce
2 tbsp mirin
1 tbsp sake
1 tbsp sesame oil, plus extra to toss
black pepper
1.5 litres Chicken stock (see page 248)
1 piece of kombu (Japanese dried kelp),
  lightly rinsed
3cm knob of fresh root ginger,
  peeled and cut into matchsticks
2–3 tbsp miso paste
200g soba noodles (Japanese buckwheat
  noodles)
150g shiitake mushrooms, stems
  trimmed and tops scored
4 spring onions, trimmed and thinly
  sliced on the diagonal
1 tsp toasted sesame seeds, to sprinkle

First, marinate the chicken. Cut the chicken breasts across the grain into thin slices. Place in a bowl and add the tamari, mirin, sake, sesame oil and a generous grinding of pepper. Give the chicken a good stir, to ensure that every piece is coated. Cover with cling film and leave to marinate in the fridge for at least 30 minutes, or preferably overnight.

For the soup base, pour the chicken stock into a medium pan and add the kombu. Bring to a simmer, cover the pan with a lid and cook gently for 5–10 minutes. Fish out and discard the kombu, which will have imparted a lovely savoury flavour to the stock. Add the ginger and stir in the miso paste. Simmer for another 3–5 minutes.

When ready to serve, bring a pot of water to the boil for the noodles. Add the mushrooms to the pan of simmering stock and cook for 2 minutes, then add the chicken strips. Cook until the chicken is just opaque through to the middle, about 1–1½ minutes. Taste and adjust the seasoning. Put the lid on the pan and turn the heat down as low as possible.

Add the noodles to the pot of boiling water and cook until they are tender but still retain a slight bite, about 3–4 minutes. Drain and immediately toss with a little sesame oil. Divide between warm soup bowls and scatter over the spring onions. Ladle the hot soup over the noodles, making sure that you divide the chicken and mushrooms evenly. Sprinkle with the sesame seeds and serve at once.

Spiced pumpkin & butter bean pot

Serves 4

1kg wedge of cooking pumpkin
  (about 750g peeled weight)
4 tbsp olive oil
1 banana shallot (or 3 regular ones),
  peeled and chopped
2 garlic cloves, peeled and finely
  chopped
sea salt and black pepper
1 tsp paprika
1 tsp ground ginger
1 tsp ground cumin
1 tsp ground turmeric
500–600ml hot Chicken stock
  (see page 248)
2 x 400g cans butter beans, rinsed and
  drained
bunch of flat leaf parsley, chopped
bunch of coriander, chopped
4 tbsp natural or Greek yoghurt, to serve

Remove the skin from the pumpkin, discard the seeds and roughly chop the flesh into 5cm cubes. Heat half the olive oil in a large saucepan and add the pumpkin, shallot, garlic and some salt and pepper. Stir over a high heat for 10 minutes until the pumpkin cubes are lightly caramelised and soft. Add the spices and stir over the heat for another couple of minutes.

Pour in the stock to cover the pumpkin and bring to a simmer. Cook for 10 minutes, then remove from the heat and leave to cool slightly. While still hot, purée the mixture in a blender until smooth and creamy. (You may need to do this in two batches.)

Return the purée to the pan and bring to a simmer over a medium heat. Tip in the butter beans and chopped herbs and heat, stirring occasionally, for 2–3 minutes until the beans are hot. Taste and adjust the seasoning.

Ladle the soup into warm bowls and add a spoonful of yoghurt. Serve with plenty of warm flatbreads.

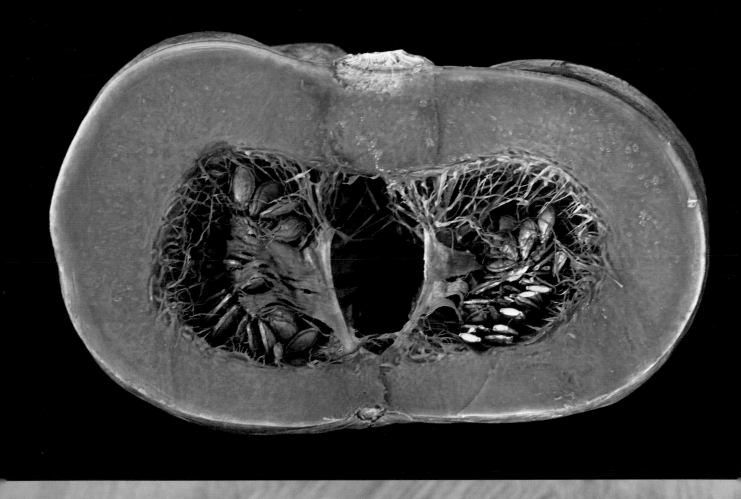

Borlotti bean minestrone

Serves 4

2 tbsp olive oil, plus a little extra to drizzle
  (optional)
2 onions, peeled and chopped
2 medium carrots, peeled and chopped
1 celery stick, trimmed and chopped
sea salt and black pepper
few thyme sprigs
1 bay leaf
80g smoked back bacon, trimmed of fat
  and chopped
2 tbsp tomato purée
2 x 400g cans borlotti beans, rinsed and
  drained
150g cherry tomatoes, halved
600–800ml Chicken stock (see page 248)
  or water
75g spaghetti, broken into small pieces
large handful of basil, finely shredded
Parmesan, for grating (optional)

Heat the olive oil in a large pan and add the onions, carrots, celery and some seasoning. Stir frequently over a medium-high heat for 6–8 minutes until the vegetables are beginning to soften. Add the thyme, bay leaf and bacon. Increase the heat slightly and cook, stirring, for another 2 minutes. Stir in the tomato purée and cook for another minute.

Tip in the borlotti beans and cherry tomatoes and then pour in the chicken stock or water to cover. Bring to a gentle simmer. Add the spaghetti and cook for 10 minutes. Taste and adjust the seasoning.

To serve, ladle into warm soup bowls and scatter over the shredded basil. If you wish, add a restrained drizzle of olive oil and grate a little Parmesan over each portion. Serve with chunks of rustic country bread.

Spiced lentil soup

Serves 4

275g split red lentils
2 tbsp olive oil
1 large onion, peeled and finely chopped
2 large garlic cloves, peeled and finely
   chopped
1 tsp ground cumin
1 tsp ground coriander
2 tsp garam masala
½ tsp ground ginger
½ tsp ground turmeric
1 tbsp tomato purée
800ml Vegetable stock (see page 249) or
   Chicken stock (see page 248)

To finish
1 tbsp olive oil (optional)
1 tsp mustard seeds (optional)
1 tsp kalonji (black onion) seeds
   (optional)
3–4 tbsp natural yoghurt
coriander leaves

Rinse the lentils in a colander and drain well. Heat the olive oil in a medium pan and add the onion and garlic. Sauté for 4–6 minutes until lightly golden. Stir in the ground spices and tomato purée and cook for another 2 minutes.

Tip in the lentils and pour in the stock to cover. Bring to the boil, then lower the heat. Simmer, uncovered, for 25–30 minutes or until the lentils are very soft, giving them a stir every now and then. You may need to top up with a little more water towards the end of cooking if the soup seems too thick. Taste and adjust the seasoning.

Ladle half of the soup into a blender and whiz to a purée, then pour back into the pan. The soup should be somewhat chunky. Adjust the consistency again if necessary, adding a little boiling water to thin it down.

For a little extra spice and fragrance if required, heat the 1 tbsp olive oil in a small pan and tip in the mustard and black onion seeds. When they begin to pop, pour the mixture over the soup and stir.

Ladle the soup into warm bowls and top with a spoonful of yoghurt and a few coriander leaves. Serve with warm Indian bread on the side.

Bacon, pea & goat's cheese omelette

Serves 4

20g butter
8 rashers of smoked streaky bacon,
  chopped
200g peas (thawed, if frozen)
few basil leaves, roughly sliced or torn
8 large eggs, beaten
150g goat's cheese log with rind,
  thickly sliced
sea salt and black pepper
Parmesan, for grating
large handful of rocket leaves
2–3 tbsp Vinaigrette (see page 250)

Preheat the grill to its highest setting. Melt the butter in a large non-stick frying pan and fry the bacon until golden brown and crisp. Toss in the peas and cook for another minute or two, then add the basil.

Pour in the beaten eggs and gently shake the pan over medium heat. As the omelette begins to set at the bottom, top with the goat's cheese. Season generously with pepper and a little salt.

Grate some Parmesan over the omelette and place the pan under the hot grill for a minute or two until the eggs are set on top. Slide onto a warm large plate.

Toss a handful of rocket leaves in vinaigrette to dress lightly, then pile on top of the omelette. Cut into wedges to serve.

Sweet potato frittata with tomato salsa

Serves 2

1 large sweet potato, about 200–250g
1 tbsp olive oil
1 shallot, peeled and finely chopped
sea salt and black pepper
4 large eggs
small handful of chives, finely snipped

Tomato salsa

250g vine-ripened plum tomatoes
2 spring onions, trimmed and thinly
    sliced on the diagonal
handful of coriander leaves, chopped
handful of rocket leaves
juice of ½ lemon
3 tbsp extra virgin olive oil
1 tbsp sesame oil
dash of Tabasco sauce
pinch of sugar (optional)

To make the salsa, halve or quarter the tomatoes and place in a large bowl. Add all the other ingredients and mix well, seasoning to taste with salt and pepper, and a pinch of sugar if you like. Set aside.

For the frittata, heat the grill to its highest setting. Peel the sweet potato and cut into 1cm cubes. Heat a non-stick omelette or frying pan (suitable for use under the grill) and add the olive oil. When hot, toss in the sweet potato and shallot, and season well with salt and pepper. Cook over a medium heat, turning occasionally, for about 4–5 minutes until the potatoes are just tender and lightly golden at the edges.

Lightly beat the eggs in a bowl, add the chives and pour over the sweet potatoes. Shake the pan gently to distribute the ingredients and cook over a low heat, without stirring, for a few minutes until the eggs are beginning to set at the bottom and around the sides.

Place the pan under the hot grill briefly until the top of the frittata has set. Try not to overcook the eggs or they will turn rubbery. Leave to stand for a minute, then run a heatproof plastic spatula around the sides of the pan and invert the frittata onto a large plate. Spoon the tomato salsa into a neat pile on top and serve immediately.

Creole spiced bean & vegetable salad

Serves 6

2 tbsp olive oil

1 onion, peeled and thinly sliced

sea salt and black pepper

200g French beans, trimmed

2 courgettes, trimmed and sliced into
   1½cm rounds

8 spring onions, trimmed and cut into
   short lengths

400g can haricot or butter beans, rinsed
   and drained

400g can cannellini beans, rinsed and
   drained

400g can chickpeas, rinsed and drained

250g cherry tomatoes, halved

bunch of flat leaf parsley, leaves only,
   roughly chopped

bunch of coriander, leaves only,
   roughly chopped

Creole spice mix

1½ tsp sweet paprika

1½ tsp dried basil

1½ tsp dried thyme

pinch of cayenne pepper, or to taste

pinch of chilli powder, or to taste

Heat the olive oil in a wide saucepan and add the onion with some salt and pepper. Stir frequently over a medium heat for 6–8 minutes until the onion is soft.

Meanwhile, combine the ingredients for the Creole spice mix in a small bowl. Add to the pan and stir for another minute or two until fragrant.

Tip the French beans, courgettes and spring onions into the pan and cook for 6–8 minutes until tender. Turn off the heat, add the canned beans and chickpeas along with the cherry tomatoes, and toss to mix.

Transfer the salad to a large bowl and stir in the chopped parsley and coriander. Serve slightly warm or at room temperature.

Fusilli salad with merguez & olives
Serves 2

150g fusilli
sea salt and black pepper
200g merguez sausages
2 tbsp olive oil
50g sun-dried tomatoes
100g pitted olives, quartered
handful of chopped mixed herbs, such
   as flat leaf parsley, chives and basil

Cook the fusilli in a pan of well salted water for about 10–12 minutes or until al dente.

In the meantime, thinly slice the sausages on the diagonal. Heat the olive oil in a frying pan and fry the sausage slices over a medium heat until golden brown. Toss through the sun-dried tomatoes and the olives. Warm through for a minute or two, then take off the heat.

Drain the pasta and toss with the sausage mix. Taste and adjust the seasoning. Stir through a handful of chopped mixed herbs and serve warm or cold. Suitable for a lunchbox.

Leftover roast chicken salad
Serves 2

200g watercress
½ roast chicken (perhaps leftover from
   yesterday's roast)
juice of ½ lemon
6 tbsp extra virgin olive oil
sea salt and black pepper
lemon wedges, to serve

Trim the watercress, removing the stalks, then wash and dry well on kitchen paper. Slice or shred the meat from the roast chicken.

For the dressing, mix the lemon juice with the olive oil, adding any pan juices from the roast chicken and salt and pepper to taste. Toss the chicken in the dressing.

Add the watercress to the chicken just before serving and toss to mix. Serve with lemon wedges on the side and a few chunks of crusty baguette. Suitable for a lunchbox.

Wild rice, basmati & smoked ham salad

Serves 4

To cook the hocks

2 smoked ham hocks, about 800g each,
    soaked overnight and drained
1 onion, peeled and halved
1 large carrot, peeled and cut into
    3 chunks
1 celery stick, trimmed and cut into
    3 pieces
handful of flat leaf parsley sprigs
handful of thyme sprigs
1 bay leaf
½ tsp black peppercorns

Salad

150g mixed basmati and wild rice
150g French beans, trimmed and halved
handful of flat leaf parsley, roughly torn
squeeze of lemon juice, to taste
3 tbsp extra virgin olive oil
black pepper

Put the ham hocks into a large pan with the onion, carrot, celery, herbs and peppercorns. Pour over enough cold water to cover the hocks and bring to the boil, then skim off any scum from the surface. Cover and simmer gently for 3–4 hours until the hocks are very tender – the meat should slide easily from the bone.

Leave the hocks to cool slightly in the poaching stock, then lift onto a plate. While still warm, peel off the skin and remove the fat. Break the meat into flakes and place in a salad bowl.

Measure 1 litre of the ham poaching stock. (You can save the rest to make a soup.) Pour the measured stock into a medium saucepan and add the basmati and wild rice. Bring to the boil, lower the heat to a simmer and cook for 20–25 minutes until the rice is tender.

Blanch the green beans in the meantime. Add them to a pan of boiling salted water and cook for 3–4 minutes until just tender. Drain and refresh under cold running water. Drain thoroughly.

When ready, drain the rice in a colander set over another pan. Place the pan lid over the colander to let the rice steam and dry out a little, then tip into the bowl containing the ham. Add the beans, parsley, lemon juice, olive oil and a generous grinding of black pepper. Toss well and serve warm, or at room temperature if you prefer.

Penne, runner beans & goat's cheese

Serves 4

300g dried penne (or other pasta shapes)
sea salt and black pepper
75g butter
1 red chilli, trimmed, deseeded and finely
   chopped
few rosemary sprigs, leaves only,
   chopped
250g runner beans, trimmed and sliced
   on the diagonal
extra virgin olive oil, to drizzle
150g soft rindless goat's cheese log
50g pine nuts, toasted

Add the pasta to a large pan of boiling salted water and cook until al dente, about 8–10 minutes.

Meanwhile, melt the butter in a large pan, add the chilli and rosemary and warm over a low heat for 1–2 minutes to let the flavours infuse. Turn up the heat, add the runner beans and cook for 3–4 minutes, stirring occasionally, until they are tender.

Drain the pasta and toss with a little olive oil, then mix with the beans. Off the heat, crumble in the cheese and toss to mix, adding a splash of boiling water if the sauce is too thick. Season with salt and pepper to taste, scatter over the pine nuts and serve.

Tabbouleh with goat's cheese

Serves 4

150g bulgar wheat
sea salt and black pepper
4 spring onions
3 ripe plum tomatoes
bunch of flat leaf parsley, chopped
bunch of mint, chopped
finely grated zest of 1 lemon
2 tbsp lemon juice
2 tbsp extra virgin olive oil, plus extra
    to drizzle (optional)
pinch of caster sugar (optional)
150g soft goat's cheese

Put the bulgar wheat into a saucepan and pour on enough water to cover by 3–4cm. Add some seasoning and bring to the boil, then reduce the heat slightly. Simmer for about 12–15 minutes until the bulgar wheat is tender but still retains a bite.

In the meantime, trim and finely slice the spring onions on the diagonal. Halve, deseed and finely chop the tomatoes and place in a salad bowl with the spring onions. Trim the herb bunches, discarding the thicker stalks, then chop them fairly finely and add to the bowl.

When it is ready, drain the bulgar wheat in a colander or sieve and leave to dry out for a few minutes. Tip into the salad bowl, then add the lemon zest and juice, olive oil, sugar if required, and seasoning to taste. Toss to mix. Crumble over the goat's cheese, and drizzle over a little olive oil if you wish, to serve.

Penne primavera

Serves 4

300g dried penne (or other pasta shapes)
sea salt and black pepper
8–10 baby leeks, white part only
4 baby fennel, trimmed
8 radishes, trimmed and halved
    lengthways
6 baby carrots, scrubbed or peeled
4 baby turnips, scrubbed and halved
4 baby courgettes, trimmed and thickly
    sliced on the diagonal
few thyme sprigs
3–4 tbsp extra virgin olive oil
juice of ½ lemon
handful of basil leaves, shredded
handful of mint leaves, shredded
3–4 tbsp freshly grated Parmesan,
    to serve (optional)

For the pasta, bring a pot of salted water to the boil. At the same time, bring a large pan of water (that will take a large steamer basket) to the boil ready to steam the vegetables. Put all the baby vegetables into your steamer basket and sprinkle over the thyme sprigs and a little sea salt.

Set the steamer basket over the pan of boiling water. Cover and steam for 6–8 minutes until the vegetables are just tender.

Meanwhile, add the pasta to the boiling salted water and cook until al dente, according to the packet instructions. Reserving a little water in the pan, drain the pasta into a colander then tip back into the pan and immediately toss with the olive oil and lemon juice.

When cooked, add the vegetables to the pasta, discarding the thyme sprigs. Toss to mix and season well to taste. Mix through the shredded herbs and divide between warm serving plates. Serve as is, or with a sprinkling of grated Parmesan.

Ratatouille

Serves 4

1 large red onion, peeled
1 small aubergine
1 red pepper, halved, cored and deseeded
1 yellow pepper, halved, cored and
   deseeded
1 large courgette
4 tbsp olive oil
few thyme sprigs
sea salt and black pepper
1 fat garlic clove, peeled and smashed
400g can chopped tomatoes
225g vine-ripened cherry tomatoes
small handful of basil leaves,
   roughly torn

Chop the vegetables into bite-sized pieces, keeping them separate. Heat the olive oil in a large pan and sauté the onion with the thyme sprigs and a little seasoning over a high heat for a minute or two.

Add the aubergine, red and yellow peppers, and the garlic. Sauté for a minute, then add the courgette and fry for another 2 minutes or so.

Tip in the canned tomatoes and add a splash of water. Now add the cherry tomatoes and bring to a simmer. Cook for 8–10 minutes until the vegetables are just tender.

Season the ratatouille with salt and pepper to taste, and sprinkle with basil before serving.

Pasta with pancetta, leek & mushrooms
Serves 4

300g dried pasta shells (conchiglie)
sea salt and black pepper
3–4 tbsp olive oil
125g pancetta, sliced
2 medium leeks, trimmed and finely sliced
250g chestnut mushrooms, trimmed and sliced
2–3 tbsp crème fraîche
bunch of flat leaf parsley, chopped

Add the pasta shells to a pot of boiling salted water and cook for 8–10 minutes or until al dente.

Meanwhile, heat the olive oil in a large frying pan and add the pancetta. Fry for a few minutes until golden brown, then add the leeks, mushrooms and a little salt and pepper. Stir over a high heat for 6–8 minutes until the leeks are tender.

Drain the pasta and immediately toss with the leeks, pancetta and mushrooms, and the crème fraîche. Season with salt and pepper to taste. Scatter over the chopped parsley to serve.

Rice noodle & smoked mackerel salad

Serves 2

65g bundle of rice noodles
100g sugar snap peas, trimmed
sea salt
1 tbsp grated fresh ginger
juice of ½ lime
1 tbsp light soy sauce
1 tbsp fish sauce
1 tbsp mirin
1 tbsp sesame oil
100g hot smoked mackerel (coated in
   peppercorns)
2 tbsp sesame seeds, toasted
1 spring onion, trimmed and finely sliced

Put the rice noodles into a large bowl, pour over boiling water to cover and leave to soak for 10 minutes. Blanch the sugar snap peas in a pan of salted water for 2 minutes until still slightly crunchy. Drain and refresh under cold running water, then slice in half, if you like.

Mix the grated ginger with the lime juice, soy sauce, fish sauce, mirin and sesame oil. Drain the noodles well, then toss with the sugar snaps and dressing.

Flake the mackerel into large pieces and scatter over the dressed rice noodles and sugar snaps. Sprinkle with the toasted sesame seeds and spring onion. Serve cold.

Spaghetti with anchovy, garlic & parsley

Serves 4

300g dried spaghetti

sea salt and black pepper

3 tbsp olive oil, plus extra to drizzle

2 garlic cloves, peeled and thinly sliced

200g pack freshly marinated anchovies,
   roughly chopped

bunch of flat leaf parsley, roughly
   chopped

freshly grated Parmesan, to serve

Cook the spaghetti in boiling salted water for 8–10 minutes or until al dente.

Heat the olive oil in a large pan, in the meantime. Add the garlic and fry over a medium heat until golden brown at the edges. Stir in the chopped anchovies.

Drain the spaghetti and tip into the pan with the garlic and anchovies. Add the chopped parsley and season to taste with salt and pepper. Toss well.

Divide among warm bowls and serve with grated Parmesan and a drizzle of olive oil.

Pappardelle, smoked trout & tomatoes

Serves 4

6 vine-ripened plum tomatoes

sea salt and black pepper

15 semi-dried tomatoes in oil (about 85g)

2 garlic cloves, peeled and roughly
  chopped

2 banana shallots (or 4 regular ones),
  peeled and roughly chopped

175ml olive oil

juice of ½ lemon

500g fresh pappardelle or tagliatelle

600g skinless smoked trout fillets, flaked
  into large chunks

Parmesan, for grating

Add the plum tomatoes to a large pan of boiling salted water and blanch for 2 minutes. Lift out with a slotted spoon to a bowl of iced water to cool for a few minutes, then remove and peel off the skins. Halve the tomatoes and squeeze out the seeds.

Put the tomatoes into a food processor along with the semi-dried tomatoes, garlic, shallots, olive oil and lemon juice. Whiz to a smooth sauce and season to taste. Pour the sauce into a pan and warm through over a medium-high heat while you cook the pasta.

Cook the pasta in boiling salted water (the pan you used for the tomatoes) for 2 minutes until al dente. Drain well, then toss with the tomato sauce and flaked trout. Divide among warm plates and grate over some Parmesan to serve.

Spaghetti vongole

Serves 4

2kg fresh palourdes (carpet shell clams)
   in the shell
sea salt and black pepper
300g dried spaghetti or linguine
2 tbsp olive oil
3 fat garlic cloves, peeled
1 banana shallot, peeled and roughly
   sliced
1 small red chilli, quartered lengthways
handful of basil stalks
75ml dry white wine
2 tbsp flat leaf parsley, finely chopped

Scrub the clams

under cold running water and discard any that do not close tightly when gently tapped on the work surface. Meanwhile, bring a large pan of salted water to the boil for the pasta. When it comes to a rolling boil, add the spaghetti and cook until it is al dente.

Cook the clams

about 6 minutes before the pasta will be ready. Heat another large pan and add the olive oil. Tip in the clams and throw in the garlic, shallot, chilli and basil stalks. Pour in the wine and cover the pan with a tight-fitting lid. Shake the pan and leave to steam for 3–4 minutes until the clams have opened. Tip the clams into a colander set over a large clean bowl. Discard any that have not opened.

Pour the clam juices

back into the pan and boil for a few minutes until thickened slightly. Throw in the parsley, then taste and adjust the seasoning. Clams are naturally salty so you may find that you only need pepper.

Drain the pasta

thoroughly. Immediately add to the sauce and toss to coat. Return the clams to the pan and toss again. Divide between warm plates and serve immediately, with chunks of crusty bread to mop up the juices.

Pan-fried crumbed fish

Serves 4

4 skinned white fish loin fillets
   (eg haddock, cod or coley), about
   170g each
75g plain flour
sea salt and black pepper
1 large egg, beaten
75g fresh breadcrumbs or Japanese
   panko breadcrumbs
3–4 tbsp olive oil
lemon wedges, to serve

Check the fish fillets for any pin-bones, removing any you find with a pair of tweezers.

Tip the flour onto a plate and season with salt and pepper, mixing well. Pour the beaten egg into a shallow dish. Scatter the breadcrumbs on another plate.

Heat the olive oil in a large frying pan. Dip the fish fillets into the seasoned flour to coat, shaking off excess. Dip into the beaten egg, and finally into the breadcrumbs to coat evenly all over. Place in the hot frying pan and fry for about 5 minutes until golden and crisp all over, turning once.

Drain the fish on kitchen paper and serve immediately, with chunky chips (see page 206), mushy peas and lemon wedges for squeezing.

Herby crayfish & prawn pilaf

Serves 4

2–3 tbsp olive oil

3 small or 2 large red onions, peeled
    and thinly sliced

250g basmati rice

finely pared zest of 2 lemons

few thyme sprigs

2 garlic cloves (unpeeled), lightly
    smashed

sea salt and black pepper

550ml hot Fish stock (see page 248)

750g live crayfish, washed

250g large raw prawns

handful of chives, finely snipped

handful of basil leaves, finely sliced

handful of chervil leaves, roughly
    chopped

Heat the oven to 190°C/Gas 5. Cut a greaseproof paper circle slightly larger than a heavy-based ovenproof pan or a cast-iron casserole. Snip a small hole in the middle of the paper to act as a steam vent.

Heat the pan with the olive oil, then sauté the onions for 4–6 minutes until they begin to soften. Stir in the rice, lemon zest, thyme, garlic and some seasoning. Stir well to toast the rice for a couple of minutes. Pour in the hot fish stock and bring to the boil. Add the crayfish to the pan and quickly cover with the greaseproof paper. Transfer the pan to the oven.

After 15 minutes, take the pan out of the oven, lift the greaseproof paper and scatter over the prawns. Re-cover with the greaseproof paper and return to the oven for 10 minutes until the rice is tender and the prawns are just cooked through and opaque. Remove from the oven and leave to stand for about 5 minutes before lifting off the paper.

Fork through the rice to distribute the crayfish and prawns evenly. Check the seasoning and stir in the chopped herbs. Serve at once.

Escabeche of mackerel

Serves 4

4 mackerel, filleted and pin-boned
sea salt and black pepper
2–3 tbsp olive oil, plus extra to oil
1 large carrot, peeled and finely sliced
1 large shallot, peeled and finely sliced
2 star anise
pinch of saffron strands
½ tsp coriander seeds, crushed
50ml white wine vinegar
150ml dry white wine
1 tbsp caster sugar
chopped coriander leaves

Season the mackerel with salt and pepper and lay in a lightly oiled wide dish. Heat the olive oil in a saucepan and add the carrot, shallot, star anise, saffron strands, crushed coriander seeds and a pinch of salt. Fry for 2–3 minutes, then add the wine vinegar, white wine and sugar. Simmer for 5 minutes, then adjust the seasoning.

Pour the hot marinade over the fish and allow to cool. Cover with cling film and chill overnight.

Serve at room temperature, scattered with chopped coriander leaves, with crusty bread on the side. The mackerel is best eaten without the skin.

Smoked mackerel & fennel salad
Serves 4

2 large fennel bulbs
2 peppered smoked mackerel fillets
1½ tbsp grainy mustard
1½ tbsp runny honey
1½ tbsp lemon juice
6–7 tbsp extra virgin olive oil
sea salt and black pepper
handful of chopped dill

Shave the fennel bulbs, using a mandolin. Immerse in iced water for 10 minutes to crisp up. Drain well and tip into a salad bowl. Flake the mackerel fillets and add to the fennel.

For the dressing, whisk together the mustard, honey, lemon juice, extra virgin olive oil and some seasoning. Add the chopped dill to the fennel and smoked mackerel with the dressing and toss well.

Herrings with mustard & dill
Serves 4

1 small cucumber, peeled and deseeded
handful of chopped dill
200g natural yoghurt
juice of ½ lemon
sea salt and black pepper
pinch of paprika
4 herrings, 250g each, cleaned
2 tbsp mustard
4–5 tbsp porridge oats
1 tsp thyme leaves
1–2 tbsp olive oil

For the sauce, peel and deseed the cucumber, then grate and squeeze out the excess water. Mix with the chopped dill, yoghurt, lemon juice, salt, pepper and paprika.

Fillet the herrings and check for pin-bones, then brush the mustard over the boned sides. Mix the oats with the thyme leaves and use to coat the herring fillets. Heat the olive oil in a non-stick frying pan and fry the fish for about a minute on each side. Serve immediately, with the sauce.

Seared tuna with swiss chard
Serves 4

4 tuna steaks, about 150g each, 2cm thick
sea salt and black pepper
1 tbsp chopped coriander leaves
olive oil, to drizzle
bunch of Swiss chard, leaves and stalks separated
2 garlic cloves, peeled and finely chopped
1 red chilli, deseeded and finely chopped

Season the tuna, sprinkle with the coriander and drizzle with olive oil. Set aside for 10 minutes. Thinly slice the chard stalks; roughly chop the leaves. In a large oiled pan, lightly fry the garlic and chilli. Add the chard stalks, seasoning and a splash of water. Cover and cook for 5 minutes. Add the leaves. Cook for 3–5 minutes until tender.

Sear the tuna in a non-stick frying pan for 1–1½ minutes each side. Rest for a few minutes, then serve with the chard.

Glazed ling with sweet 'n' sour shallots

Serves 4

4 skinless ling, cod or whiting fillets,
    about 170g each
a little olive oil, to oil
60ml light soy sauce
2 tbsp dark soy sauce
100ml white wine vinegar
50g soft brown sugar
1 tsp coriander seeds, lightly crushed
1 tsp black peppercorns, lightly crushed
3cm knob of fresh root ginger, peeled
    and finely grated
400g small shallots, peeled
75ml dry white wine
150ml Fish stock (see page 248)
small handful of chives, snipped

Lay the fish fillets in a lightly oiled large baking dish and set aside. Put the soy sauces, wine vinegar and sugar in a saucepan and stir over a low heat to dissolve the sugar. Increase the heat and tip in the coriander seeds, peppercorns and ginger. Boil for 8–10 minutes until the liquid has reduced by half. Leave to cool completely.

Heat the oven to 180°C/Gas 4. Blanch the shallots in a pan of boiling water for 10 minutes until tender, then drain.

Pour the soy mixture over the ling fillets and cook in the oven for 5 minutes until the sauce begins to caramelise. Scatter the blanched shallots around the fish and pour on the white wine and fish stock. Return the dish to the oven and bake for a further 6–8 minutes until the fish is just cooked through.

Transfer the fish to a warm plate, using a fish slice. Cover with foil and set aside to rest in a warm place for 5–10 minutes. Meanwhile, tip the onions and liquor into a pan and boil for 10 minutes until reduced to a sticky sauce.

Place the fish on warm plates and spoon over the shallots and sauce. Garnish with snipped chives and serve with steamed rice and stir-fried pak choi, if you wish.

Glazed salmon with spinach & radish salad

Serves 4

4 lightly smoked salmon fillets,
   125–150g each
100g baby spinach leaves, washed
   and dried
8–10 radishes, washed, trimmed and
   finely sliced

Marinade
3 tbsp honey
1 tbsp lemon juice
2 tbsp light soy sauce
1 tsp Dijon mustard
½ tsp grated fresh root ginger

Dressing
1 tbsp grated fresh root ginger
3 tbsp rice wine vinegar
2 tbsp light soy sauce
2 tbsp sesame oil
2–3 tbsp tahini

Remove the skin from the salmon and check carefully for pin-bones, pulling out any with kitchen tweezers. Place the fillets side by side in a shallow dish. For the marinade, mix the ingredients together in a bowl, then pour over the salmon to coat. Cover with cling film and leave to marinate in the fridge for 30 minutes to allow the flavours to permeate.

For the dressing, whisk together all the ingredients in a bowl and set aside.

Heat the oven to 230°C/Gas 8. Arrange the spinach leaves on individual plates and top with the radish slices.

Lift the salmon from the marinade and arrange on a lightly oiled baking tray. Cook in the oven for 4–6 minutes until medium rare, basting after 2 minutes. The fish should feel slightly springy when pressed.

Place a salmon fillet in the middle of each plate and drizzle the ginger and tahini dressing over the salad to serve.

Tomato & olive crusted trout fillets

Serves 4

4 skinless trout fillets, about 130g each
sea salt and black pepper
1–2 tbsp olive oil, plus extra to oil
100g fresh breadcrumbs
1 garlic clove, peeled and crushed
30g sun-dried tomatoes, chopped
30g pitted black olives, chopped
handful of basil leaves

Heat the oven to 200°C/Gas 6. Lightly season the trout fillets with salt and pepper and place on a lightly oiled baking tray, skinned side up.

For the crust, in a bowl, mix the breadcrumbs with the garlic, sun-dried tomatoes, olives and 1–2 tbsp olive oil. Roughly chop the basil leaves and add them to the bowl. Toss to mix and season with salt and pepper to taste.

Spread the crust over each trout fillet, patting down lightly with the back of the spoon. Bake for 10–12 minutes until the crust is golden and crisp. Serve at once, with minted new potatoes and a leafy salad.

Sticky baked chicken drumsticks

Serves 5

olive oil, to drizzle
10 chicken drumsticks
sea salt and black pepper

Glaze
6 tbsp honey
3 tbsp fish sauce
1½ tbsp light soy sauce
juice of 1½ lemons
3 tbsp rice wine vinegar
1½ tbsp sesame oil

Heat the oven to 200°C/Gas 6. Lightly oil a large baking dish. Season the drumsticks with salt and pepper and arrange in the dish in a single layer. Drizzle over a little olive oil and bake in the hot oven for 20 minutes.

Make the glaze in the meantime. Mix all the ingredients together in a small bowl until evenly combined.

Take the chicken out of the oven and pour over the glaze, to coat each drumstick. Return to the oven and bake for another 20–30 minutes, turning several times, until the chicken is tender and nicely glazed.

Let the chicken rest for 5 minutes before serving. Serve with steamed rice and purple sprouting broccoli or green beans.

Beef burgers with beetroot relish & cucumber raita

Serves 4

600g good-quality lean beef mince
1 tsp smoked paprika
pinch of cayenne pepper
sea salt and black pepper
olive oil, to cook and drizzle
250g cherry tomatoes on the vine
splash of balsamic vinegar
4 Iceberg lettuce leaves, trimmed
    (optional)
handful of wild rocket leaves (optional)

Beetroot relish
250g cooked beetroot in natural juices,
    drained
3 tbsp capers, rinsed and drained
handful of flat leaf parsley, roughly
    chopped
2 tbsp balsamic vinegar
3 tbsp olive oil

Cucumber raita
1 large cucumber
handful of mint leaves, chopped
3–4 tbsp natural yoghurt
squeeze of lemon juice, to taste

Put the beef mince into a large bowl and add the paprika, cayenne, ½ tsp salt (or less to taste) and ½ tsp pepper. Mix well with your hands, then shape into 4 neat patties. Place on a plate or tray, cover with cling film and chill for at least 30 minutes to set the shape.

Make the beetroot relish in the meantime. Roughly chop the beetroot and place in a food processor along with the capers, parsley, balsamic vinegar and olive oil. Pulse until the mixture is roughly chopped – you don't want to purée the beetroot. Season to taste and transfer to a bowl.

For the cucumber raita, peel the cucumber and quarter lengthways. Scrape out the seeds with a spoon and discard. Roughly chop the flesh and place in a bowl. Add the chopped mint and toss with enough yoghurt to bind. Add the lemon juice and season with salt and pepper to taste.

Heat the barbecue or heat a drizzle of olive oil in a non-stick frying pan. Brush the burgers with olive oil and cook on the barbecue, or pan-fry allowing 3½–4 minutes on each side for medium burgers. Remove to a warm plate and leave to rest for a few minutes. Add the tomatoes to the barbecue or pan and drizzle with a little olive oil and balsamic vinegar. Cook for 1–2 minutes until the tomatoes are soft but still retain their shape.

Serve the burgers with the tomatoes, beetroot relish and cucumber raita. For a neat presentation, spoon the raita into lettuce cups and garnish with a handful of rocket.

Lamb kebabs with peppers & tomatoes

Serves 4

500g lean lamb leg steaks
1 large red pepper
1 large yellow pepper
8 chestnut mushrooms
8 cherry tomatoes, skinned if preferred
olive oil, to drizzle

Herb paste
finely grated zest and juice of 1 lemon
2 garlic cloves, peeled and finely
   chopped
½ tsp dried oregano
½ tsp dried mint
½ tsp dried thyme
¼ tsp dried ground rosemary
½ tsp dried tarragon
1 tbsp olive oil
sea salt and black pepper

Cut the lamb steaks into 2.5cm cubes and place in a bowl. Stir together all the ingredients for the herb paste and pour over the lamb. Toss well to coat the pieces evenly. Cover the bowl with cling film and leave to marinate in the fridge for several hours or overnight. Soak 6–8 bamboo skewers in cold water for at least 20 minutes.

Halve the peppers, remove the core and seeds, then cut into 2.5cm pieces. Thread the peppers, lamb, mushrooms and cherry tomatoes alternately onto the soaked bamboo skewers.

Heat the barbecue or place a griddle pan over a high heat. Drizzle a little olive oil over the skewers and sprinkle with some salt and pepper. Barbecue or grill the skewers for 2½–3 minutes on each side. Leave to rest for a minute or two, then serve with side salads of your choice.

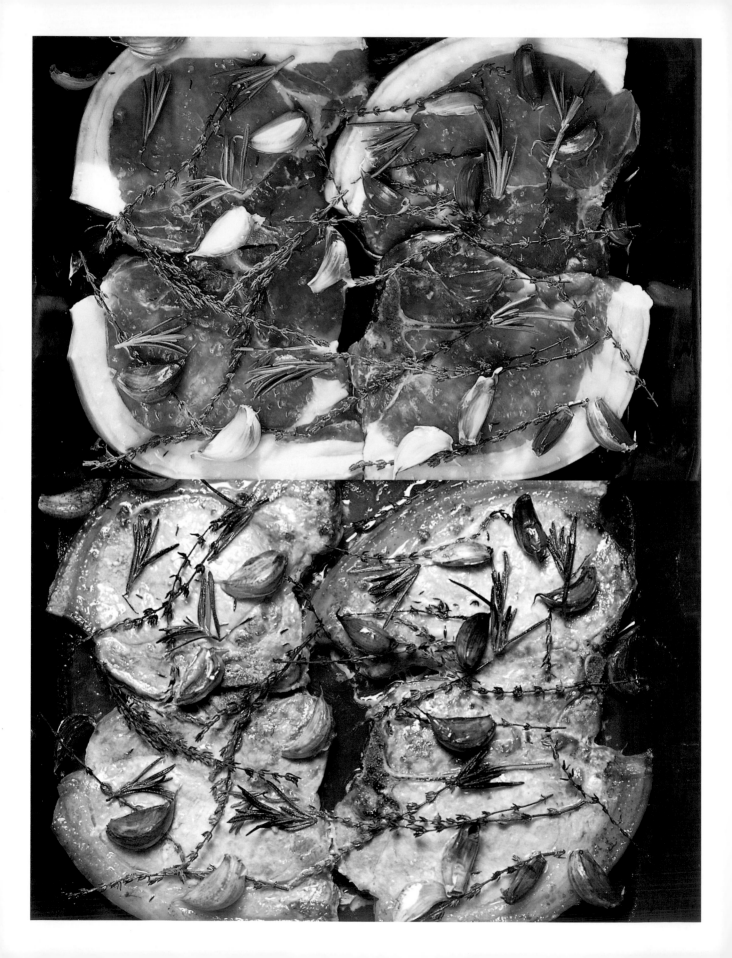

Baked pork chops with a piquant sauce

Serves 4

4 pork chops, about 250g each
a little olive oil, plus extra to drizzle
few thyme sprigs
few rosemary sprigs, leaves only
½ head of garlic, separated into cloves
  (unpeeled)
sea salt and black pepper

Sauce

3 tbsp olive oil
1 large onion, peeled and finely chopped
1 red pepper, deseeded and finely chopped
1 red chilli, deseeded and finely chopped
200g chestnut mushrooms, trimmed and
  finely sliced
400g can chopped tomatoes
sea salt and black pepper
1 tsp caster sugar

Heat the oven to 200°C/Gas 6. Place the pork chops in a large, lightly oiled baking dish and scatter over the thyme sprigs, rosemary leaves, garlic cloves and salt. Drizzle with a little olive oil and bake for 20 minutes or until the pork chops are cooked through.

Make the sauce in the meantime. Heat the olive oil in a wide pan and add the onion, red pepper, chilli and mushrooms. Stir over a high heat for 3–4 minutes until the vegetables begin to soften. Tip in the tomatoes. Season with salt and pepper and add the sugar and a splash of water. Simmer for 10–12 minutes until the onions are tender and the sauce has thickened. Taste and adjust the seasoning.

Take the chops out of the oven and leave to rest in a warm place for 5 minutes. Then pour any pan juices into the sauce and reheat. Ladle a generous amount of sauce over the chops to serve.

Italian sausages with lentils

Serves 4

olive oil, to cook

200g smoked bacon lardons

1 onion, peeled and finely chopped

1 medium carrot, peeled and cut into
   1cm cubes

3 bay leaves

500g Castelluccio or Puy lentils, rinsed
   and drained

sea salt and black pepper

1 large garlic clove, peeled and smashed

12 Italian sausages

100ml dry white wine

handful of flat leaf parsley, leaves
   chopped

Heat a little olive oil in a heavy-based saucepan and fry the lardons until lightly golden, about 5 minutes. Add the onion, carrot and bay leaves, stir well and cook over a medium heat for 5–6 minutes until the onions begin to soften.

Tip in the lentils, stir well and pour in enough water to cover. Bring to the boil, lower the heat and simmer, covered, for 25–30 minutes until most of the liquid has been absorbed and the lentils are tender. Season generously with salt and pepper.

Cook the sausages in the meantime. Heat a little olive oil in a heavy-based frying pan. Add the garlic and cook for a minute. Add the sausages and pan-fry for about 5 minutes, turning occasionally, until lightly golden. Deglaze the pan with the white wine and bring to the boil. Lower the heat to a simmer, and leave the sausages to braise for 15–20 minutes until cooked through.

With a pair of tongs, transfer the sausages to the lentils, nestling them among the vegetables and lentils and adding the pan juices. Reheat for a few more minutes.

Divide the lentils and sausages among warm shallow bowls. Sprinkle generously with chopped parsley and a grinding of black pepper, then serve.

kids' favourites

Lunchbox dips & dunkers

Serves 4–6

Smoked mackerel pâté

250g smoked mackerel fillets

2 tbsp horseradish cream

5 tbsp reduced-fat crème fraîche

2 tbsp lemon juice, or to taste

black pepper

Minted chickpea purée

400g can chickpeas, rinsed and drained

4 tbsp natural yoghurt

2 tbsp lemon juice, or to taste

sea salt and black pepper

handful of mint leaves, chopped

To serve

raw vegetable sticks, such as carrots, celery, cucumber, red and yellow peppers

cooked shelled prawns tossed with a drizzle of olive oil and thyme (optional)

To make the fish pâté, flake the smoked mackerel, checking for pin-bones, and place in a food processor. Pulse a few times to break the fish apart. Add half the horseradish cream, crème fraîche, lemon juice and some black pepper (you won't need to add salt) and pulse again until smooth. Taste the mixture and add more horseradish cream, crème fraîche and lemon juice until you are happy with the flavour and seasoning. Spoon the mixture into a lunchbox or plastic container and chill.

For the chickpea purée, put the chickpeas, yoghurt, lemon juice and some seasoning into a food processor. Blend until smooth. Transfer the mixture to a bowl and taste for seasoning, adding more lemon juice, salt and pepper as necessary. Stir through the chopped mint and chill in a lunchbox or plastic container.

Pack a selection of raw vegetable sticks in a separate container to serve with the dips. If liked, pack some prawns in another container. Add some breadsticks or pita bread, too. Follow with fresh fruit or yoghurt. The lunch must be packed in an insulated cooler bag with ice blocks to keep it chilled, especially if prawns are included.

Turkey brochettes with red pepper salsa

Serves 4–5

500g skinless, boneless turkey breasts
sea salt and black pepper
2 red onions, peeled
1 yellow pepper
1 orange pepper
olive oil, to brush

Marinade
1 tbsp lime juice
1 tbsp olive oil
½ tsp smoked paprika
½ tsp celery salt
½ tsp cornflour
pinch of cayenne pepper
dash of Tabasco sauce (optional)
dash of Worcestershire sauce

Red pepper salsa
250g jar roasted red peppers in olive oil
1 small red onion, peeled and finely
    chopped
4 spring onions, trimmed and finely
    chopped
handful of coriander leaves
juice of 1 lime
½ tsp honey, to taste

Cut the turkey into 2.5–3cm cubes. Whisk together all the ingredients for the marinade in a large bowl, adding some salt and pepper. Add the turkey and toss well to coat. Cover with cling film and leave to marinate in the fridge for at least 30 minutes or overnight. Soak 4–5 bamboo skewers in cold water for at least 20 minutes.

Cut the onions into bite-sized chunks, similar in size to the turkey cubes. Halve, core and deseed the peppers, then cut into 2.5–3cm squares. Thread the peppers, onions and turkey cubes alternately onto the skewers. Place on a lightly oiled tray, cover with cling film and chill until ready to cook.

For the salsa, drain the peppers and chop finely. Place in a bowl and add all the rest of the ingredients. Toss together and season with salt and pepper to taste. (The salsa is now ready to eat, or it can be chilled for up to an hour.)

To cook, heat a griddle pan or the grill until hot. Brush the brochettes with a little olive oil and cook for 10–15 minutes, turning several times. The turkey should feel just firm when lightly pressed; don't overcook or it will be dry. Serve immediately, with the salsa.

Chicken burgers with sweet potato wedges

Makes 6 small burgers

3 tbsp olive oil
1 medium sweet onion, peeled and finely chopped
2 garlic cloves, peeled and finely crushed
sea salt and black pepper
350g minced skinless, boneless chicken breasts
1 large egg
handful of herbs, such as flat leaf parsley and chives, chopped

Sweet potato wedges
3 medium sweet potatoes, peeled
olive oil, to drizzle
honey, to drizzle (optional)

To serve
6 mini buns, preferably wholemeal, split
1 large ripe avocado
squeeze of lemon juice
1 large beef tomato, thinly sliced
Tomato ketchup (see page 114)

Heat 1 tbsp olive oil in a pan and sweat the onion and garlic with some seasoning for 4–6 minutes until soft but not brown. Tip into a large bowl and leave to cool completely.

Add the chicken, egg and seasoning, then stir in the chopped herbs, until evenly distributed. Cover with cling film and chill for an hour to allow the mixture to firm up.

Shape the mixture into 6 small patties, with moist hands; try not to compact them. Place on a tray lined with baking parchment. Chill until ready to cook.

Heat the oven to 200°C/Gas 6. Line a baking tray with baking parchment. Cut the sweet potatoes into wedges and place in a large bowl with a drizzle of olive oil and some seasoning. Spread out in a single layer on the baking tray and bake for 15–20 minutes until golden brown at the edges. If you wish, drizzle with a little honey. Keep warm in a low oven.

To cook the burgers, heat 2 tbsp olive oil in a large frying pan or griddle pan. When hot, add the patties and fry for 4 minutes on each side until golden brown and just cooked through. (Don't press them with a spatula as they cook or you'll squeeze out the juices.) Remove to a warm plate and leave to rest.

Lightly toast the buns on both sides. Halve, peel and stone the avocado, then slice thinly, squeezing over a little lemon juice to prevent them discolouring. Sandwich each bun with a chicken burger and a few slices of avocado and tomato. Serve immediately, with the sweet potato wedges and ketchup.

Crusted fish fillets with tomato ketchup

Serves 4

4 thick, skinless cod fillets, about
   130–140g each
1–2 tbsp olive oil, plus extra to oil
50g fresh white breadcrumbs
finely grated zest of 1 lemon
25g Parmesan, freshly grated
1–2 thyme sprigs, leaves stripped
sea salt and black pepper

Tomato ketchup
1 tbsp olive oil
1 sweet onion, peeled and chopped
2 garlic cloves, peeled and chopped
½ tsp fennel seeds, crushed
½ tsp coriander seeds, crushed
500g ripe plum tomatoes, skinned and
   chopped
300ml tomato juice or water
50g light brown sugar
1 tbsp red wine vinegar
few basil sprigs

For the ketchup, heat the olive oil in a pan and sweat the onion with the garlic over a medium-low heat for 4–6 minutes until softened. Add the crushed fennel and coriander seeds with some seasoning and cook, stirring, for half a minute. Add the chopped tomatoes, tomato juice or water, sugar, vinegar and basil and simmer gently for 25–30 minutes or until the mixture is thick and the tomatoes are sweet and pulpy. Adjust the seasoning and sweetness, adding a little more sugar or vinegar if needed.

Whiz in a blender or food processor to a smooth purée, then pass through a fine sieve into a bowl and leave to cool.

Heat the oven to 220°C/Gas 7. Check the cod fillets carefully for pin-bones, removing any that you come across with kitchen tweezers. Place the fillets, skinned side up, on a lightly oiled baking tray.

In a bowl, mix together the breadcrumbs, lemon zest, Parmesan, thyme and a little salt and pepper to taste. Stir in a little olive oil to combine.

Spread the breadcrumb mixture evenly on top of each fish fillet. Bake in the oven for 7–8 minutes until the topping is golden brown and crisp, and the fish flesh is opaque.

Transfer the fish to warm plates and serve with the home-made ketchup, mash and peas or broccoli.

Sausage & beans
Serves 2

4 Toulouse sausage
2 tbsp olive oil
few thyme sprigs
2 garlic cloves, peeled and finely sliced
400g can mixed beans, drained and rinsed
400g can chopped tomatoes
sea salt and black pepper
pinch of sugar (optional)

Fry the sausages in a wide, heavy-based pan with the olive oil and a few thyme sprigs until lightly coloured on all sides. Add the garlic and cook for 3–4 minutes, stirring occasionally, until the sausages are golden brown.

Tip in the beans and chopped tomatoes. Bring to a simmer, partially cover and stew for 10–12 minutes, by which time the sausages should be cooked through.

Season with salt, pepper and a pinch of sugar if the tomato sauce is too sharp. Serve in bowls with chunks of crusty bread.

115

Rigatoni with yellow & green courgettes

Serves 4–5

250g dried rigatoni (or other pasta
    shapes)
sea salt and black pepper
2 large green courgettes, trimmed
2 large yellow courgettes, trimmed
3–4 tbsp olive oil
1 garlic clove, peeled and finely crushed
handful of basil leaves
Parmesan, for grating

Add the pasta to a pot of boiling salted water and cook according to the packet instructions until al dente.

Meanwhile, halve the courgettes lengthways and slice thickly. Heat a large frying pan and add the olive oil. Tip in the crushed garlic and sauté for just less than a minute.

Add the courgettes with a pinch of salt and a grinding of pepper. (If your pan is not large enough, cook the courgettes in two batches.) Fry over a high heat for 3–4 minutes until the courgettes are just tender and lightly golden brown around the sides. Take off the heat.

When ready, drain the pasta and immediately toss with the courgettes and basil. Taste and adjust the seasoning. Divide among warm plates and grate over some Parmesan to serve.

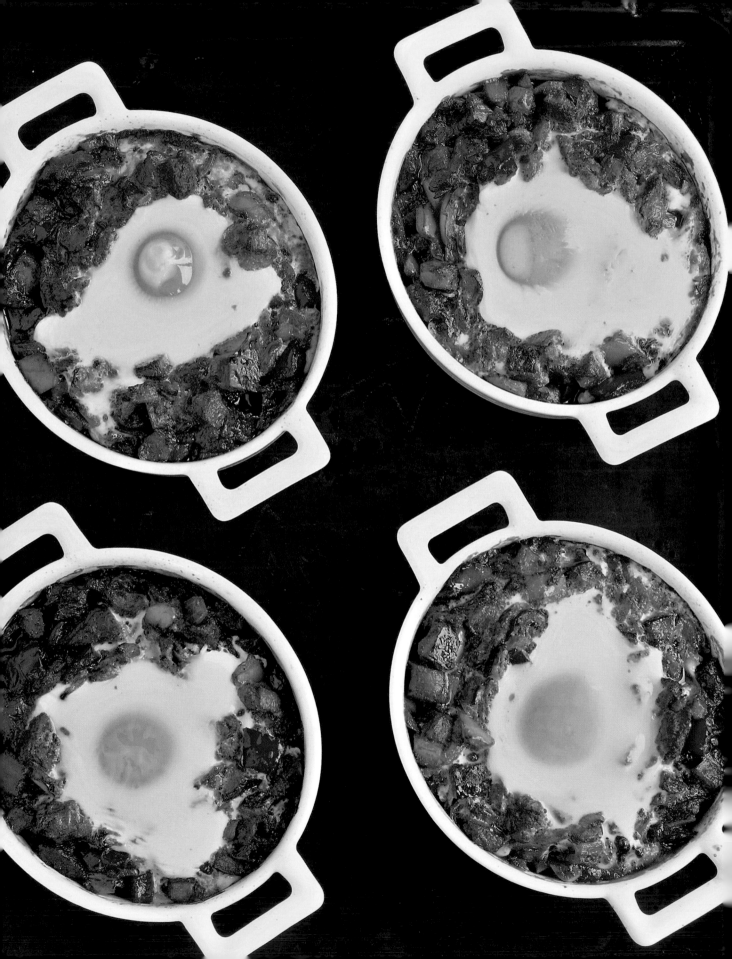

Baked eggs with ratatouille

Serves 4

1 large red onion, peeled
1 small aubergine, trimmed
1 large red pepper, halved, cored and
    deseeded
1 large green pepper, halved, cored and
    deseeded
1 large courgette, trimmed
3–4 tbsp olive oil
sea salt and black pepper
2 garlic cloves, peeled and finely
    chopped
¼–½ tsp mild chilli powder (optional)
1 tsp ground cumin
1 tsp sweet paprika
250g canned chopped tomatoes
4 large eggs

Heat the oven to 200°C/Gas 6. Chop the onion, aubergine, peppers and courgette into 1.5cm cubes, keeping them separate. Put a large frying pan over a high heat and add the olive oil, onion and a little seasoning. Sauté for 2 minutes, then add the aubergines, peppers and garlic and fry for another minute. Tip in the courgettes and sauté for another minute or two.

Add the ground spices and chopped tomatoes. Bring to a simmer and cook for 8–10 minutes until the vegetables are tender. Taste and adjust the seasoning.

Divide the ratatouille between four individual shallow ovenproof dishes. Make an indentation in each portion with the back of a spoon, then crack an egg into each one. Sprinkle the top of each egg with a pinch each of salt and pepper.

Stand the dishes on a large baking tray and bake for 10–12 minutes until the egg whites are set but the yolks are still runny in the middle. Serve immediately, with some wholemeal toasts on the side.

Fromage frais, yoghurt & plum ripple

Serves 4–6

4 ripe plums, about 500g
½ tsp ground cinnamon
2–3 tbsp caster sugar, to taste
1 star anise (optional)
300ml natural yoghurt
300ml fromage frais
2–3 tbsp icing sugar, or to taste

Halve the plums, remove the stones and roughly chop the flesh. Toss with the cinnamon and 2 tbsp caster sugar. Place a wide frying pan over a high heat, tip in the plums and add the star anise, if using. Sauté for 4–6 minutes until the plums are soft, moistening with a splash of water if necessary. Taste for sweetness, adding more sugar if the plums are too tart. Discard the star anise.

Transfer the cooked plums to a blender or food processor and whiz until smooth. For a really smooth purée, pass through a fine sieve to remove any pulpy bits. Cool completely.

Spoon the yoghurt and fromage frais into a large bowl and add the icing sugar. Beat lightly to mix, then ripple through all but 2 tbsp of the plum purée. Spoon into individual glasses or plastic tumblers and swirl the remaining plum purée on top. Serve at once.

Knickerbocker glory

Serves 6

140g packet strawberry jelly
3 tbsp boiling water
400ml cold water
300g ripe cherries, pitted
50ml orange juice, mixed with
    25ml water
50g caster sugar
1 small ripe mango
100g strawberries, hulled
2 clementines
500ml good-quality vanilla ice cream
50g amaretti biscuits
40g chocolate buttons

Break the jelly into small pieces and put into a bowl. Pour on the boiling water and microwave on high for 1–1½ minutes. Stir until completely dissolved, then mix in the cold water. Pour the jelly into a shallow bowl or loaf tin and chill overnight to set.

Place the cherries in a non-stick pan, sprinkle with the diluted orange juice and sugar and cook over a high heat for 1–2 minutes until the cherries are soft but still holding their shape. Remove from the heat and leave to cool.

Put six tall glasses or plastic tumblers into the refrigerator to chill, ready for serving.

Peel the mango and cut the flesh away from the stone, then chop into 1cm cubes. Quarter or slice the strawberries depending on size. Peel the clementines and slice horizontally into thin rounds.

Unmould the jelly onto a board and roughly chop into small pieces. Lightly crush the amaretti biscuits in a bowl with the end of a rolling pin.

To assemble, layer the cherries, mango, clementines, chopped jelly, ice cream, strawberries and chocolate buttons in the chilled glasses or tumblers. Top with a final scoop of ice cream and sprinkle with the crushed amaretti biscuits. Serve immediately.

food to share

starters

Warm black pudding & quail's egg salad

Serves 4

24 quail's eggs, at room temperature
200g black pudding
2–3 tbsp olive oil
75ml Vinaigrette (see page 250)
200g mixed salad leaves
sea salt and black pepper

Bring a small pan of water to a gentle boil. Lower the quail's eggs into the water and cook for 2 minutes, then drain and refresh in a bowl of cold water. Peel off the shells and halve the eggs lengthways, if you like.

Thickly slice the black pudding into rounds. Heat the olive oil in a non-stick frying pan and fry the black pudding slices for 2–3 minutes on each side. Add the quail's eggs to the pan to warm through briefly. Pour in the vinaigrette and quickly remove the pan from the heat.

Tip the pan contents into a large bowl containing the salad leaves. Toss lightly and season with a little salt and pepper. Pile onto individual plates to serve.

Prawn, feta & watermelon salad

Serves 4

200g raw prawns, peeled and deveined
2 tbsp olive oil
pinch of cayenne pepper
sea salt and black pepper
1.5kg ripe seedless watermelon
50g wild rocket leaves, washed
120g feta cheese
1 tbsp toasted mixed seeds, such as
   pumpkin and sunflower seeds
   (optional)

Dressing
2 tbsp lime juice
½ tsp caster sugar
4 tbsp extra virgin olive oil

Marinate the prawns by tossing them together with 1 tbsp olive oil, a pinch of cayenne and some salt and pepper in a bowl. Cover with cling film and leave to marinate in the fridge for 10–15 minutes.

Cut the watermelon into wedges, then cut off the skin and slice the flesh thinly. Layer the watermelon slices on a large serving platter, interleaving them with rocket leaves. Crumble over the feta and grind over some black pepper.

Place a large frying pan, preferably a non-stick one, over a medium heat and add 1 tbsp olive oil. Tip in the prawns and fry for about 2 minutes until they turn opaque, flipping them over after a minute or so. Transfer to a plate and leave to cool slightly while you make the dressing.

Whisk the dressing ingredients together and season to taste. Add the prawns to the platter and scatter over the seeds, if using. Drizzle with the dressing and serve at once.

Clams with aïoli

Serves 6–8

2–2.5kg fresh clams, cleaned

3–4 tbsp olive oil, plus extra to drizzle

3 banana shallots (or 6 medium shallots),
   peeled and thinly sliced

few thyme sprigs

4 bay leaves

splash of dry white wine

small bunch of flat leaf parsley, leaves
   only, chopped

Aïoli

100ml Mayonnaise (see page 250)

2 garlic cloves, peeled and finely crushed

pinch of paprika

sea salt and black pepper

First, make the aïoli.
Mix the mayonnaise with the crushed garlic, paprika and salt and pepper to taste until evenly combined. Set aside.

To cook the clams,
you will need one very large or two smaller heavy-based saucepans. Heat the olive oil in the pan(s), add the shallots and sauté for 3–4 minutes to soften. Tip in the clams, add the thyme and bay leaves with a splash of wine and cover with a tight-fitting lid. Give the pan a good shake and let the clams steam for 4–5 minutes until the shells have opened. Take the pan off the heat.

Using a slotted spoon,
transfer the clams to serving bowls, throwing away any that haven't opened.

Stir enough aïoli
into the pan juices to thicken them (about 3–4 tbsp), then add the chopped parsley. Spoon the sauce over the clams and drizzle with a little olive oil to serve. Hand round the rest of the aïoli separately.

Sautéed scallops with sweetcorn salsa

Serves 4

12 scallops, shelled and cleaned
½ tsp medium curry powder
2 tbsp olive oil
small handful of rocket leaves

Sweetcorn salsa
400g can sweetcorn, drained
200g cherry tomatoes, quartered
1 red chilli, deseeded and finely chopped
1 red onion, peeled and finely chopped
2 spring onions, trimmed and finely sliced
3 tbsp sesame oil
handful of coriander, roughly chopped
juice of 2 limes
dash of light soy sauce
sea salt and black pepper

For the salsa, combine all the ingredients in a saucepan and stir over a medium heat for 2 minutes to warm through.

Halve the scallops horizontally into two discs. Mix the curry powder with 1 tsp sea salt and sprinkle over the scallops.

Heat a large frying pan over a high heat and add the olive oil. Pan-fry the scallops for 1 minute each side until golden brown at the edges, turning them in the same order you put them in the pan to ensure they cook evenly; don't overcook.

Spoon the salsa onto warm plates and arrange the scallops on top. Scatter over a few rocket leaves and serve.

Smoked trout, orange & rocket salad

Serves 4

3 oranges
4 tbsp extra virgin olive oil
sea salt and black pepper
200g wild rocket leaves, washed
2 hot smoked trout fillets, about
   125g each

To segment the oranges, cut off the top and bottom of one and stand it upright on a board. Cut along the curve of the fruit to remove the skin and white pith, exposing the flesh. Now hold the orange over a sieve set on top of a bowl and cut out the segments, letting each one drop into the sieve as you go along. Finally, squeeze the membrane over the sieve to extract as much juice as possible. Repeat with the remaining oranges, then tip the segments into another bowl.

For the dressing, add the olive oil and a little seasoning to the orange juice that you've collected in the bowl and whisk to combine.

Add the rocket to the orange segments, then flake the smoked trout into the bowl. Add the dressing and toss gently with your hands. Pile onto individual plates and serve with pumpernickel or rye bread.

Artichoke, asparagus & tomato tart

Serves 6

Onion purée
olive oil, to cook
6 onions, peeled and finely chopped
sea salt and black pepper
4 tbsp single cream

Tart
500g ready-made puff pastry
flour, to dust
150g asparagus tips
12 quail's eggs
150g ready-cooked artichoke hearts,
    cut into wedges
150g cherry tomatoes, halved
½ small red onion, peeled and finely
    sliced
small handful of chives, chopped
3–4 tbsp Vinaigrette (see page 250)
few rocket leaves, to garnish

For the onion purée, heat a little olive oil in a pan, add the onions and season well. Cover and cook over a low heat, stirring occasionally, for 10–15 minutes until the onions are very soft. Meanwhile, heat the oven to 200°C/Gas 6.

Roll out the pastry thinly on a lightly floured surface and cut out 6 discs, using a 13–15cm plate or saucer as a guide. Lay the pastry discs on a large baking sheet and prick all over with a skewer. Place another heavy baking sheet on top of the pastry discs to weigh them down. Bake for 15 minutes until brown and crisp. Transfer to a wire rack to cool.

Add the cream to the onions and bring to a simmer. Tip the mixture into a blender or food processor and whiz to a fine paste. For a very smooth purée, push the onion paste through a sieve. Leave to cool.

Blanch the asparagus tips in a pan of boiling salted water for 2 minutes until tender. Remove with tongs and refresh in a bowl of iced water, then drain and tip into a large bowl.

Add the quail's eggs to the boiling water in the pan carefully, and cook for 2 minutes, 10 seconds. This will leave the eggs with runny yolks. Refresh under cold running water and peel off the shells.

Add the artichokes, tomatoes, red onion and chives to the asparagus, drizzle with the vinaigrette and toss to mix.

Spoon a little onion purée over the centre of the pastry discs and pile the vegetables on top. Halve the quail's eggs and arrange on the vegetables. Scatter a few rocket leaves over, sprinkle with a little salt and pepper and serve.

Baked stuffed figs with goat's cheese

Serves 4

8 ripe figs
100g soft goat's cheese
handful of chives, finely snipped
good-quality balsamic vinegar, to drizzle
few thyme sprigs, leaves stripped
2 tbsp toasted pine nuts

Trim off the tip from each fig, then cut a cross through the top, cutting about halfway down. Squeeze the base of the figs to open out the top quarters like a flower.

Stuff the figs with the goat's cheese, sprinkle with snipped chives and drizzle with balsamic vinegar. Scatter over the thyme leaves and pine nuts.

Stand the figs on a large piece of foil. Bring up the sides and fold together to seal the parcel. You can either bake the figs in a hot oven, preheated to 200°C/Gas 6, or on a barbecue. They should take about 10–12 minutes.

Unwrap the parcel and serve the figs immediately, as a starter, or as an accompaniment or to round off a meal.

fish

Easy lobster thermidor

Serves 4

2 freshly cooked lobsters
Parmesan, for grating
small handful of chives and chervil,
   chopped

Sauce
100g crème fraîche
2 egg yolks
1 tsp dry English mustard
sea salt and black pepper

Uncurl the lobster tails and place them flat on a board. Using a strong pair of kitchen scissors, snip along the bottom shells, then use a large knife to cut the tails into two halves. Remove the flesh and place back into the shells, the other way around.

To prepare the claws, pull out the small claw to release the blade, then crack open the shells of the thick claws with the back of a knife. Gently pull out the flesh and place on a baking tray, along with the lobster tails.

Preheat the grill to its highest setting. For the sauce, mix all the ingredients together, then spoon over the lobster tails and claws. Grate over a little Parmesan and grill for 3–4 minutes until golden. Serve immediately, with a sprinkling of chopped herbs.

Grilled sardines with chermoula

Serves 4

8 very fresh sardines, gutted and cleaned
sea salt and black pepper
little olive oil, to drizzle

Chermoula
2 tsp cumin seeds
2 tsp coriander seeds
2 garlic cloves, peeled and roughly
   chopped
1 tsp sweet paprika
finely grated zest and juice of 1 small
   lemon
4–5 tbsp extra virgin olive oil
small handful of coriander, chopped

To make the chermoula, toast the cumin and coriander seeds in a pan over a low heat until fragrant. Tip into a mortar and add a pinch each of salt and pepper. Grind to a fine powder, then add the garlic and grind the mixture to a paste. Stir in the rest of the ingredients.

Score the sardines lightly on both sides at 1cm intervals and place in a shallow dish. Pour half of the chermoula mixture over the fish and rub the marinade into the scored skin. Cover with cling film and leave to marinate in the fridge for at least 1 hour, or up to 4 hours.

Preheat the grill to high or heat up the barbecue. Season the sardines with a little salt and pepper and oil lightly. Place them on a wide oiled baking tray or in a sandwich-style barbecue rack if barbecuing. Grill for 4–5 minutes each side, basting with the pan juices as you turn them halfway; allow 3 minutes each side on the barbecue.

Transfer the sardines to a warm platter, spoon over the remaining chermoula and serve with rice or zesty couscous.

Salmon with mediterranean flavours

Serves 4

4 skinned salmon fillets, about 200g
  each
50g sun-dried tomatoes in oil, halved
  if large
handful of basil leaves
50g pitted black olives
3 large garlic cloves, peeled and thinly
  sliced
sea salt and black pepper
olive oil, to drizzle

Heat the oven to 200°C/Gas 6. Place the salmon fillets on a board, skinned side down. Use an apple corer to make 6 small holes in each fillet.

Flatten the sun-dried tomatoes and place a basil leaf, an olive and a sliver of garlic on each one. Roll up and use to stuff the holes in the salmon. Season with salt and pepper.

Place the salmon fillets on a lightly oiled baking tray. Drizzle with olive oil and bake for 6–8 minutes until medium-rare – the thickest part will feel slightly springy when pressed. Transfer to warm plates and serve with the tomato salad and country bread.

Salmon baked with herbs &
caramelised lemons

Serves 6–8

1 whole salmon, about 1.6 kg, scaled,
   gutted and washed
olive oil, to cook and drizzle
sea salt and black pepper
2 bay leaves
few sprigs each of rosemary, thyme, basil,
   sage and parsley
1 head of garlic (unpeeled), halved
   horizontally, then broken into cloves
2–3 lemongrass stalks, split in half
   lengthways and bruised with the back
   of a knife
1 large or 3 small lemons, thickly sliced
5–6 star anise
1 tsp mixed (or black) peppercorns
Mayonnaise (see page 250), to serve
   (optional)

Trim a little off the tail and fins of the salmon with kitchen scissors and pat dry with kitchen paper. Pat the cavity dry as well. Score the skin of the salmon on both sides with a sharp knife, at 1–2 cm intervals. Rub all over with olive oil, salt and pepper.

Tear two sheets of foil, large enough to envelope the salmon easily. Lay one on top of the other on the work surface and scatter the bay leaves, herb sprigs, garlic and lemongrass over the middle of the foil. Lay the fish on the bed of herbs and tuck some of the flavourings into the cavity.

Fry the lemon slices in a little olive oil for 2–3 minutes until caramelised around the edges, seasoning them with salt and pepper. Allow to cool slightly. Tuck the caramelised lemon slices around the fish, placing some in the cavity and some on top. Scatter the star anise and peppercorns over and around the fish, putting some inside the cavity. Drizzle the salmon with a little olive oil. Heat the oven to 190°C/Gas 5.

Fold the edges of the foil tightly together over the salmon to seal, leaving some space in the parcel for steam to surround and cook the fish. Put the salmon parcel in the roasting tin and cook in the centre of the oven for 25–30 minutes, depending on the thickness of the salmon. Remove from the oven and without unwrapping the foil parcel, rest the fish for 5–10 minutes.

Unwrap the salmon and peel off the skin with a palette knife. Use the back of a spoon to slide the fish off the bone. Serve individual portions garnished with the caramelised lemons and accompanied by a side salad and mayonnaise, if you like.

Pan-fried sea bass with sorrel sauce

Serves 4

4 sea bass fillets, skin on, about 175g
  each
olive oil, to cook and drizzle
sea salt and black pepper
2 heads of broccoli, cut into florets
handful of sorrel leaves, shredded

Fish velouté
knob of butter
2 small shallots, peeled and finely
  chopped
100ml dry white wine
100 ml dry vermouth
200ml Fish stock (see page 248)
150ml double cream

Make the fish velouté. Heat the butter in a wide saucepan. Stir in the shallots and sauté gently for about 10 minutes until soft but not coloured. Pour in the wine and vermouth and boil until reduced by half. Then add the stock, return to the boil and reduce by half. Stir in the cream and simmer gently until the sauce is the consistency of pouring cream. Season to taste with salt and pepper and strain the sauce through a fine sieve.

Check the bass fillets for small pin-bones, removing any with tweezers. Using a sharp knife, lightly score the skin at 1cm intervals. Heat a little olive oil in a large frying pan until hot. Season the fish fillets and place them in the pan, skin side down. Fry, without moving, for 2–3 minutes until the skin is crisp and the fish is cooked two-thirds of the way through. Turn the fillets and cook the other side for about 30 seconds.

While the fish is cooking, blanch the broccoli in boiling salted water for 2 minutes and drain well. Drizzle with a little olive oil and season with salt and pepper. Keep warm.

Transfer the fish to a warm plate and lightly cover with foil. Pour the fish velouté into the pan and scrape up the sediment with a wooden spoon to deglaze the pan. Simmer for a few minutes, then add half of the shredded sorrel and take off the heat.

Divide the broccoli among warm serving plates and lay the sea bass fillets on top. Pour the sauce around the plate and garnish with the remaining shredded sorrel.

Monkfish with curried mussels

Serves 4–6

4–6 monkfish tail fillets, about 150g each
500g mussels, cleaned with beards
   removed
few thyme sprigs
2 bay leaves
75ml dry white wine
1 large carrot, peeled and chopped
1 leek, trimmed and chopped
½ celeriac, peeled and chopped
3 tbsp olive oil
5 tsp curry powder
2 pinches of saffron strands
sea salt and black pepper
400g baby spinach, washed
knob of butter
200ml double cream
handful of chives, chopped

Trim the monkfish fillets if necessary, removing any grey membrane. Heat the oven to 180°C/Gas 4.

Heat a large saucepan until hot, then add the mussels, a couple of thyme sprigs, the bay leaves and white wine. Cover the pan with a tight-fitting lid and give it a good shake. Cook for about 3–4 minutes, shaking once or twice, until the mussels have opened. Strain and reserve the juices. Remove the mussels from their shells and set aside; discard any unopened ones.

Sauté the vegetables in 1 tbsp olive oil until soft. Sprinkle with 1 tsp curry powder and the saffron. Add a thyme sprig, tip in the mussel juice and simmer until reduced by half.

Meanwhile, mix the remaining 4 tsp curry powder with 1 tsp salt. Pat the monkfish tails dry with kitchen paper and dust with the curry/salt mix. Heat 2 tbsp olive oil in an ovenproof frying pan and fry the monkfish fillets for 2–3 minutes until golden brown. Transfer the pan to the oven for 4–5 minutes to finish off the cooking. The fish is ready when it feels just firm.

Wilt the spinach gently in a warm pan with a knob of butter for about 1–2 minutes while the fish is in the oven. At the same time, pour the cream into the sautéed vegetables and bring to a gentle simmer. Add the mussels to warm through, then finally mix in the chives and season with salt and pepper to taste.

Divide the spinach among warm plates and spoon over the creamy mussel mixture. Thickly slice the monkfish and arrange on top. Serve at once.

Black bream with peas 'bonne femme'

Serves 6

6 black bream fillets, skin on, about
   175g each
sea salt and black pepper
small handful of basil leaves
olive oil, to drizzle

Peas 'bonne femme'
olive oil, to cook
250g unsmoked bacon lardons
150g pearl onions, peeled
few thyme sprigs, leaves only
600g fresh or frozen peas
   (thawed, if frozen)

Check the fish for small bones, removing any that you find with tweezers. Score the skin at 1cm intervals. Season with salt and pepper and place a few basil leaves on the flesh side. Place each bream fillet on a large piece of cling film and drizzle with olive oil. Wrap up to enclose the fillets in the cling film, twisting the ends tightly to seal.

For the peas, heat a little olive oil in a frying pan and fry the lardons for 8–10 minutes until golden brown and crisp. Remove and drain on kitchen paper. Add the onions and thyme to the pan and cook on a medium heat, stirring occasionally, for 10 minutes until the onions are tender.

In the meantime, bring a large pan of water to the boil, then reduce the heat to a low simmer. Add the wrapped bream fillets and gently poach for about 10 minutes until the fish is opaque and cooked through. If the centre is not cooked through, poach for a further 2–3 minutes.

Add the peas and bacon to the onions and cook for 2–3 minutes until the peas are tender. Season well.

Divide the peas 'bonne femme' among six warm plates. Unwrap the bream fillets and place one on top of each pile of vegetables, skin side up. Drizzle with a little olive oil and sprinkle with a little sea salt. Serve immediately.

John dory with sweet onions & kale

Serves 4

400g kale, stalks removed, roughly
    shredded
sea salt and black pepper
4 tbsp olive oil
2 large onions, peeled and sliced
2 tsp caster sugar
knob of butter
2 tbsp sherry vinegar
4 John Dory fillets, about 175g each,
    skinned
4 tbsp Fish or Chicken stock (see
    page 248)

Add the kale to a pan of boiling salted water and blanch for 3–4 minutes. Drain in a colander, refresh under cold running water and set aside.

Heat a sauté pan and add half the olive oil. Toss in the onions, season and sprinkle with the sugar. Add a splash of water and cook over a medium-high heat, stirring from time to time, for about 8 minutes until the onions are caramelised.

Add the blanched kale and a knob of butter to the onions. Toss well over the heat, then pour in the sherry vinegar and let bubble until it has reduced right down.

Heat a large frying pan with the remaining oil. Season the fish fillets and fry for 2–2½ minutes until the fish is cooked two-thirds of the way through. Turn over and add the stock. Cook for 30–40 seconds until the fish is just cooked.

Divide the onions and kale among four serving plates. Place the fish fillets on top and pour over the juices from the pan. Serve immediately.

Red mullet with orange & fennel

Serves 4

8 red mullet fillets, about 100g each
2 large oranges
1 large or 2 medium heads of fennel
2 red chillies
2 tsp fennel seeds
olive oil, to drizzle
4 splashes of dry white wine

Heat the oven to 200°C/Gas 6. Cut 4 large squares of
baking parchment. Fold each square in half to form a crease in the
middle, then open out and set aside. Check the red mullet fillets for
pin-bones, removing any with kitchen tweezers.

To prepare the oranges, slice off the top and
bottom, then cut off the peel and pith following the curve of the fruit.
Now, holding the orange over a sieve set on top of a bowl to catch the
juice, cut along the membranes to release each segment. Squeeze out
any juice from the pulp and discard.

Trim the fennel, then slice thinly. Halve, deseed and
thinly slice the chillies into rings.

Divide the fennel slices, orange segments and
chilli slices among the parchment squares, piling them on one side of
the crease. Lay two red mullet fillets on each pile. Scatter over the
fennel seeds and drizzle with a little olive oil. Fold the other side of the
parchment over the filling to enclose.

To seal each parcel, make small folds all along the
edges to hold them together. Just before the final fold, tilt the parcel
slightly and pour in a splash of wine and a quarter of the orange juice.
Repeat with the remaining parcels.

Place the parcels on two large baking sheets and
bake for 10 minutes until the fish is just firm, opaque and cooked
through. Put a parcel on each warm plate and bring to the table
to cut open.

Tandoori spiced halibut with cucumber

Serves 4

4 skinned halibut fillets, about 150g each
1 tbsp tandoori or hot Madras curry paste
1 tbsp olive oil
1 tsp caster sugar
150g tub natural yogurt
2 cucumbers, peeled
handful of mint leaves, chopped
squeeze of lime juice
1–2 tbsp vegetable oil

Heat the oven to 200°C/Gas 6. Lay the halibut fillets on a plate. Mix the curry paste with the olive oil and sugar. Stir in all but 3 tbsp of the yogurt. Coat the fish with the spiced yogurt and set aside.

Cut the cucumbers lengthways using a swivel vegetable peeler into long wide strips, avoiding the seeds in the middle. Toss with the reserved 3 tbsp yogurt, chopped mint and lime juice.

Heat an ovenproof pan and add the vegetable oil. Scrape off the excess marinade from the halibut fillets and place them in the hot pan, reserving the marinade. Sear for 1–1½ minutes on each side until golden brown.

Spoon the marinade over the fish and place the pan in the oven for a few minutes to finish cooking. Transfer to warm plates, drizzle over the pan juices and serve with the cucumber salad.

Saffron-marinated bream with sweet & sour peppers

Serves 4

4 black bream fillets, about 140g each
2½ tbsp olive oil
generous pinch of saffron strands
sea salt and black pepper
basil sprigs, to garnish

Sweet and sour peppers

6 red peppers
2 tbsp olive oil
1 tsp caster sugar
small splash of red wine vinegar

Trim the bream fillets to neaten and pull out any pin-bones with kitchen tweezers. Mix the olive oil and saffron strands together in a wide dish. Add the fish fillets and toss well to coat. Grind over some pepper, cover with cling film and leave to marinate in the fridge for 20 minutes.

To prepare the peppers, halve, core and deseed, then cut into thin slices. Heat the olive oil in a large frying pan or wok, add the peppers and stir-fry over a high heat for 2–3 minutes until they begin to soften. Season with salt and pepper and add the sugar and a small splash of wine vinegar. Let bubble for a minute or two until the vinegar has cooked down and the peppers are tender. Take off the heat and set aside; keep warm.

To cook the fish, heat a wide non-stick frying pan until hot. Season the bream fillets with salt and pepper and fry, skin side down, for about 2 minutes until the skin is golden brown and crisp. Flip the fillets over and fry the other side for a minute until the flesh is opaque.

Divide the peppers between warm plates and top with the bream fillets. Serve immediately, garnished with basil.

Brill with creamed cabbage & bacon

Serves 4

4 tbsp olive oil

6 rashers of unsmoked streaky bacon, derinded and chopped

1 large carrot, peeled and diced

½ celeriac, peeled and diced

½ Savoy cabbage, cored and finely shredded

200ml double cream

sea salt and black pepper

4 brill fillets, about 150g each, skinned

large knob of butter

juice of ½ lemon

large handful of flat leaf parsley, chopped

Heat 2 tbsp olive oil in a large pan. Add the chopped bacon and fry for a few minutes, then stir in the carrot and celeriac. Cover the pan with a tight-fitting lid and cook for 8–10 minutes over a medium heat until the celeriac turns translucent.

Add the shredded cabbage and cook for 3–4 minutes, then pour in the cream. Simmer for a few minutes until the cream has thickened and the cabbage is tender. Season well with salt and pepper and keep warm.

Meanwhile, heat a sauté pan and add the remaining olive oil. Season the fish with salt and pepper. When the pan is hot, add the fish, skinned side down, and fry for 1½ minutes until golden brown on the underside.

Flip the fish over and add the butter to the pan. Squeeze over the lemon juice and let bubble gently for 1–2 minutes. Toss in the parsley and spoon the herby butter over the fish. Take off the heat.

Spoon the creamed cabbage into the middle of four warm plates and top with the brill fillets. Spoon any remaining pan juices over the fish and serve.

poultry & game

Mango, avocado & smoked chicken salad

Serves 4

2 medium, firm but ripe mangoes
2 ripe avocados
squeeze of lemon juice
300–350g smoked chicken breasts
200g mixed salad leaves, such as rocket,
    mâche, baby chard or amaranth
2 tbsp pine nuts, toasted (optional)

Dressing
2 tbsp orange juice
2 tbsp lemon juice
1 tbsp wholegrain mustard
2 tbsp extra virgin olive oil
2 tbsp avocado oil (or olive oil)
sea salt and black pepper

Peel the mangoes and cut the flesh away from the stone into thin slices. Arrange on four serving plates.

Halve the avocados and remove the stones. Peel off the skin and slice the flesh into strips. Squeeze over a little lemon juice to stop the flesh discolouring, then arrange over the mango slices.

Cut the chicken into thin slices and divide between the plates. Neatly pile the salad leaves in the middle.

For the dressing, whisk the ingredients together in a bowl, seasoning with salt and pepper to taste.

Spoon the dressing over the salad and serve, topped with a handful of toasted pine nuts if you like.

Stuffed chicken breasts in parma ham

Serves 4

4 large chicken breasts, about 170–200g
8 sage leaves
5 heaped tbsp ricotta
sea salt and black pepper
8 Parma ham slices
1½ tbsp olive oil
handful of thyme sprigs

Cut a deep slit along one side of each chicken breast, without slicing right through, then open it out like a book. On a clean chopping board, finely chop 4 sage leaves, then mix into the ricotta and season with salt and pepper to taste.

Lay two Parma ham slices on the board, overlapping them slightly. Put a sage leaf in the middle and lay an open chicken breast on top. Spoon a quarter of the ricotta mixture onto the middle of the chicken, then fold the sides together again, to enclose the filling. Now wrap the Parma ham slices around the stuffed chicken breast. Wrap in cling film. Repeat with the rest of the chicken breasts and chill for 1–2 hours to firm up slightly.

Heat the oven to 180°C/Gas 4 and place a roasting pan in the oven to heat up. Remove the cling film from the chicken. Heat a heavy-based frying pan and add the olive oil. When hot, fry the Parma-wrapped chicken, in batches if necessary, for 2 minutes on each side until browned.

Lay a few thyme sprigs on each chicken breast, then place in the hot roasting pan. Cook in the oven for 12–15 minutes, depending on size, or until the meat feels just firm when lightly pressed.

Rest the chicken, covered with foil, in a warm place for 5–10 minutes. Slice each stuffed breast thickly on the diagonal and arrange on warm plates. Serve with steamed greens and light mashed potatoes or a zesty couscous.

Griddled spring chicken & vegetables on focaccia

Serves 4

2 spring chickens or poussins, about
   450g each
few rosemary sprigs, leaves only
3–4 garlic cloves, halved, with skin on
olive oil, to drizzle
sea salt and black pepper
2 large courgettes, trimmed
1 small aubergine, trimmed
1 large yellow pepper
1 large red pepper
few thyme sprigs
1 large (or 2 medium) focaccia loaves

Balsamic dressing
6 tbsp olive oil
3 tbsp balsamic vinegar

Carve out the chicken breasts and legs (or get your butcher to do this). Put them into a large bowl with the rosemary and 2 garlic cloves. Drizzle generously with olive oil and season well with pepper. Set aside to marinate.

Cut the courgettes into 1cm thick rounds. Slice the aubergine into rounds of a similar thickness. Halve, core and deseed the peppers, then cut into wedges. Place the vegetables in a bowl, add the remaining garlic and thyme and toss with a generous drizzle of olive oil. Season with salt and pepper.

For the dressing, mix the olive oil and balsamic vinegar together and season with salt and pepper to taste. Set aside.

Heat a griddle pan until it is almost smoking. You may need to cook the vegetables in batches. Using tongs, place them on the griddle and cook for about 6–8 minutes, turning halfway through cooking. Remove to a plate and set aside.

Season the chicken with salt and cook on the griddle, allowing about 3–4 minutes each side for the breasts, 5–6 minutes each side for the legs. Check it is cooked through – the meat will be firm and the juices should run clear when the thickest part is pierced with a skewer. Transfer to a plate and keep warm.

Cut the focaccia into four 10–12cm squares. If very thick, slice them in half horizontally. Griddle for 20 seconds on each side to warm through – watch closely as they burn easily. Brush with a little olive oil if you wish and place on warm plates.

Spoon the griddled veg onto the bread and top each serving with a chicken breast and leg. Spoon over the balsamic dressing and serve immediately.

Chicken with petits pois à la française

Serves 4

1 large chicken, about 1.5–2kg
3 tbsp plain flour
sea salt and black pepper
2–3 tbsp olive oil
2 carrots, peeled and cut into 1cm cubes
2 celery sticks, cut into 1cm cubes
1 large onion, peeled and finely chopped
2 garlic cloves, peeled and chopped
few thyme sprigs
2 bay leaves
150ml dry white wine
800–900ml Chicken stock (see page 248)
handful of flat leaf parsley, chopped

Petit pois à la française

2 tbsp olive oil
150g small pearl onions, peeled
few thyme sprigs
1 bay leaf
100ml Chicken stock (see page 248)
500g young, tender peas, preferably
    fresh (thawed, if frozen)
50g butter, cut into cubes
2 baby gem lettuce, shredded

Joint the chicken into eight pieces.
Season the flour with salt and pepper and toss the chicken pieces in it to coat all over. Heat a little olive oil in a wide shallow pan and fry the chicken pieces, in two batches, over a medium heat until golden brown on all sides. Remove the chicken with a slotted spoon and set aside on a plate.

Add the carrots, celery, onion, garlic, thyme and bay
leaves to the pan. Stir and cook over a medium heat for 4–5 minutes until the vegetables are beginning to soften. Pour in the white wine, scraping the bottom of the pan with a wooden spoon to deglaze. Return the chicken pieces to the pan, nestling them among the vegetables, and pour in enough stock to cover. Bring to the boil, then reduce the heat to a low simmer. Skim off any scum that rises to the surface, put the lid on the pan and simmer gently for 30–40 minutes until the chicken is tender.

With a pair of tongs, remove the chicken from
the pan and set aside. Strain the stock through a fine sieve, pushing with the back of a wooden spoon to extract as much juice from the vegetables as possible; discard the vegetables. Return the stock to a clean, wide pan. Skim off any excess fat from the top of the liquid, then allow to bubble for 10–15 minutes until reduced and thickened.

Cook the petit pois in the meantime.
Heat the olive oil in a large, shallow pan. Add the pearl onions, thyme and bay leaf and sauté over a medium heat for 5 minutes. Add the stock, peas and some salt and pepper. Simmer gently for 10 minutes until the vegetables are tender. Stir in the butter, a few knobs at a time, to enrich and help thicken the sauce. Finally, mix through the lettuce and heat briefly until wilted.

Return the chicken to the pan and reheat gently
in the sauce for a few minutes. Serve with the peas and a generous sprinkling of chopped parsley.

Herb buttered turkey with citrus breadcrumbs

Serves 6–8

1 large oven-ready turkey, about 5–5.5kg
sea salt and black pepper
2 large onions, peeled and halved
1 orange, halved
1 head of garlic (unpeeled), halved
  horizontally
few bay leaves
few thyme sprigs
olive oil, to drizzle

Herb butter
small bunch of flat leaf parsley, chopped
small bunch of tarragon, chopped
1 tbsp thyme leaves
250g butter, softened to room temperature
1 black truffle (optional)

Citrus breadcrumbs
½ loaf of day-old bread, about 300g,
  crusts removed
grated zest of 1 orange
grated zest of 1 lemon
olive oil, to cook
50g pancetta (about 7–8 rashers),
  chopped
½ onion, peeled and finely diced
few thyme sprigs
200g pine nuts
150g butter, cut into cubes
squeeze of lemon juice

For the herb butter, mix the chopped herbs into the softened butter. If using the truffle, finely slice and chop, then mix into the herb butter. Season well and spoon the flavoured butter into a piping bag.

Holding the turkey with one hand and starting from the neck flap, use the fingers of your other hand to loosen the skin over the breasts without tearing the skin. Move your hand towards the lower side of the breast and towards the thighs and separate the skin from the meat. You want to create a large pocket with which to stuff the herb butter.

Pipe the herb butter into the pockets over the turkey breasts and thighs. Gently massage over the skin to spread the herb butter evenly.

Heat the oven to 220°C/Gas 7. Open up the cavity of the turkey, season with salt and pepper and stuff with the onions, orange, garlic, bay leaves and thyme sprigs. Tuck the legs under the neck skin to secure them in place, or tie with kitchen string.

Place the turkey, breast side up, in a large roasting tray. Drizzle with a little olive oil and season well with salt and pepper. Roast for 10–15 minutes until the skin is crisp and golden. Lower the oven setting to 180°C/Gas 4 and cook for approximately 30 minutes per kg, basting occasionally.

To test that the turkey is cooked, skewer the thickest part of the thigh and check that the juices are running clear, not at all pink.

Meanwhile, make the breadcrumbs. Tear the bread roughly and whiz to coarse crumbs in a food processor. Add the orange and lemon zests and season well. Pulse a few times until well mixed.

Heat a little olive oil in a large frying pan and fry the pancetta for a minute. Toss in the onion, thyme and pine nuts. Cook for 3–4 minutes before adding the butter around the edge of the pan. Allow the butter to foam and turn a golden brown before adding the breadcrumbs. Mix well and cook, tossing frequently, for 5 minutes until the crumbs are nicely toasted and golden. Squeeze over a little lemon juice, discard the thyme and adjust the seasoning. Keep warm.

When the turkey is cooked, cover loosely with foil and leave to rest for at least 20 minutes. Carve the breast and thighs and serve with the citrus breadcrumbs, gravy and vegetables of your choice.

Duck breast with spring greens & gooseberry sauce

Serves 6

3 tbsp Szechwan peppercorns
sea salt and black pepper
6 duck breasts with skin, about 175g each
150g gooseberries
125g caster sugar
250ml water
finely pared zest of ½ lemon
150ml dry red wine
150ml Chicken (or duck) stock
   (see page 248)
3 tbsp gooseberry conserve or honey
few knobs of butter
400g spring greens, cored and finely
   shredded

Toast the peppercorns in a dry pan until fragrant, then tip into a pestle and mortar and add a little salt and pepper. Lightly crush the peppercorn mix. Score the skin of the duck breasts in a criss-cross pattern, then coat with the spice mixture.

Place the duck breasts, skin side down, in a dry ovenproof pan and cook over a very low heat to render down most of the fat. This may take 10–15 minutes. Heat the oven to 200°C/Gas 6.

Put the gooseberries, sugar, water and lemon zest in a pan and bring to a low simmer. Poach gently for 2–3 minutes, then remove from the heat and set aside to cool.

For the sauce, boil the red wine in a pan for 7–8 minutes until reduced by half. Pour in the stock and again, reduce by half.

Turn up the heat under the duck breasts and fry until the skin is crisp. Turn them over and seal the other side for 1–2 minutes. Transfer the pan to the hot oven and cook for 8–10 minutes for medium-rare duck – it should be slightly springy when pressed.

In the meantime, stir the gooseberry conserve into the sauce and add a knob of butter for shine. Drain the gooseberries and discard the lemon zest, then add the fruit to the sauce and warm through. Taste and adjust the seasoning.

When ready, transfer the duck breasts to a warm plate and set aside to rest for 10 minutes in a warm place. Wilt the spring greens with a couple of knobs of butter in a hot pan. Season well, then divide among warm serving plates. Thickly slice the duck breasts on the diagonal and fan out on top of the spring greens. Spoon the sauce over and around to serve.

Honey-glazed partridge with bashed neeps & cabbage

Serves 2

2 oven-ready partridges, about 300g each
sea salt and black pepper
2 tbsp olive oil
6 garlic cloves (unpeeled)
few rosemary sprigs
few thyme sprigs
2–3 tbsp honey

Bashed neeps
1 large swede, about 550g
15g butter

Sautéed cabbage
½ head of Savoy cabbage, core removed
    and shredded
1½ tbsp olive oil
squeeze of lemon juice, to taste

For the bashed neeps, peel the swede and cut into 3–4cm chunks. Cook in salted water to cover for about 15 minutes until quite soft. Meanwhile, blanch the cabbage in another pan of salted water for 2–3 minutes. Drain and refresh under cold running water, then drain again and set aside.

Drain the swede and return to the pan. Add the butter and crush with a potato masher, seasoning with a little more salt and pepper to taste. (For a smooth mash, whiz in a food processor, then return to the pan.)

Season the partridges with salt and pepper and heat up a frying pan. When hot, add the olive oil, garlic, rosemary and thyme. Sear the partridges for 1½–2 minutes on each side until nicely browned. Drizzle the honey over the birds and add a good splash of water to the pan. Cook, basting frequently, for 6–8 minutes until the partridge breasts feel slightly springy when pressed, indicating that they're medium rare. Transfer to a warm plate and rest for a few minutes while you reheat the vegetables.

Warm up the bashed neeps, giving the mixture a few stirs. For the cabbage, heat the olive oil in a pan, then add the blanched cabbage and toss until piping hot. Adjust the seasoning with salt, pepper and a little lemon juice.

Pile the bashed neeps and sautéed cabbage onto warm plates and sit the braised partridges alongside.

Venison pie with sweet potato topping

Serves 4–5

600g haunch of venison
sea salt and black pepper
3 tbsp plain flour
3–4 tbsp olive oil
2 leeks, white part only, sliced thickly
150g baby onions, peeled
250g small Chantenay carrots, scrubbed
250g chestnuts mushrooms, halved
1 large rosemary sprig, leaves only
150ml red wine or port
650ml Chicken stock (see page 248)
150g new potatoes, scrubbed

Sweet potato topping

500g sweet potatoes
350g Desirée potatoes
20g butter
50g double Gloucester cheese, grated
2 large egg yolks

Cut the venison into 2.5–3cm chunks. Season the flour with salt and pepper and use to coat the venison. Heat 2 tbsp olive oil in a large flameproof casserole and fry the meat in batches until evenly browned, about 2 minutes each side. Transfer to a bowl; set aside.

Add the leeks, onions and carrots to the casserole with a little more oil and stir over a medium heat for 4–5 minutes until lightly coloured. Add the mushrooms and rosemary and cook for a minute. Pour in the wine, scraping the bottom of the pan with a wooden spoon to deglaze. Bubble until reduced right down.

Pour in the stock and bring to a simmer. Return the venison, with any juices released, to the pan. Partially cover with a lid and gently braise for 40–50 minutes until the venison is tender, giving the mixture a stir every once in a while.

About 15 minutes before the venison will be ready, slice the new potatoes into 1cm thick rounds. Season and fry in a little olive oil in a wide non-stick frying pan until golden brown on both sides. Add to the casserole to finish cooking. Once the potatoes and venison are tender, remove the pan from the heat and let cool slightly.

For the topping, peel all the potatoes and cut into 5cm chunks. Cook in a pan of salted water for 15 minutes or until tender. Drain well and mash with a potato ricer back into the pan. While still hot, add the butter, cheese and some seasoning. Mix well to combine. Cool slightly, then mix in the egg yolks.

Heat the oven to 220°C/Gas 7. Tip the venison mixture into a large pie dish or a shallow cast-iron pan and top with the mash. Rough up the surface with a fork. Bake for 20 minutes until the topping is golden brown and the filling is bubbling around the sides. Grind over some pepper and serve.

Mixed vegetable stir-fry

Serves 4

2 carrots, peeled
2 celery sticks, trimmed
½ red pepper, cored and deseeded
½ yellow pepper, cored and deseeded
½ green pepper, cored and deseeded
2 tbsp vegetable oil
2 tbsp sesame oil
1 garlic clove, peeled and chopped
200g bean sprouts
1 tbsp dark soy sauce
3 tbsp oyster sauce
toasted sesame seeds

Slice the carrots, celery and peppers, keeping them separate. Heat a wok until very hot, then add the vegetable and sesame oils. Add the garlic and the sliced carrots and stir-fry for 30 seconds.

Toss in the sliced peppers and stir-fry for another 30 seconds, then add the sliced celery and bean sprouts and toss over the heat for another 30 seconds.

Add the soy sauce and oyster sauce and mix well. Scatter with toasted sesame seeds and serve.

Sautéed spinach with nutmeg
Serves 4–6

2 tbsp olive oil
600g baby leaf spinach, washed
sea salt and black pepper
grated nutmeg

Heat the olive oil in a large pan. Tip in the spinach leaves and stir over a high heat until just wilted. (You may need to cook the spinach in two batches if your pan is not wide enough.) Season with salt, pepper and a little grated nutmeg and serve immediately. An excellent base for fish, vegetarian or beef dishes.

Crunchy broccoli & cauliflower gratin
Serves 4

1 small cauliflower, cut into florets
sea salt and black pepper
1 small broccoli, cut into florets
200ml crème fraîche
2 large egg yolks
oil, for oiling
50g hazelnuts, toasted and lightly
    crushed
Parmesan, for grating

Heat the oven to 220°C/Gas 7. Add the cauliflower to a large pan of boiling salted water and blanch for 1 minute. Tip in the broccoli and cook for another 2 minutes. Drain well and tip into a bowl.

Beat the crème fraîche with the egg yolks and some salt and pepper. Pour over the vegetables and toss well, then tip into an oiled large gratin dish. Scatter over the lightly crushed hazelnuts and top with a generous grating of Parmesan. Bake for 10 minutes or until the topping is golden brown. For a crisp topping, flash under a hot grill for a few minutes before serving.

Purple sprouting broccoli with thai flavours
Serves 4

400g purple sprouting broccoli
1 small red chilli, deseeded and finely
    chopped
2 tbsp sesame oil
1½ tbsp fish sauce
juice of 1 lime
½–1 tsp caster sugar
1 tbsp sesame seeds, toasted

Cut the broccoli into even lengths. For the dressing, mix the chilli with the sesame oil, fish sauce, lime juice and sugar.

Cook the broccoli in a steamer for 4 minutes until tender and bright green. As soon it is cooked, transfer to a warm plate and spoon over the dressing. Sprinkle with the toasted sesame seeds and serve immediately.

meat

Veal piccata

Serves 4

3 tbsp olive oil
1 head of garlic (unpeeled), halved
   crossways
4 British veal chops, about 270–300g
   each and 2.5–3cm thick
sea salt and black pepper
1 rosemary sprig
handful of thyme sprigs
200ml dry white wine
2 tbsp capers, drained
100ml crème fraîche

Heat the olive oil in a wide, heavy-based pan and add the garlic halves, cut side down. Allow the garlic to infuse the oil over a medium-low heat for a minute, then increase the heat.

Season the veal chops with salt and pepper and add to the pan. Throw in the herbs and fry the veal for 1½–2 minutes on each side until golden brown. Remove the veal from the pan and leave to rest on a warm plate for 5 minutes.

Pour off the excess oil from the pan, then add the wine, scraping the bottom to deglaze. Bring to the boil and let bubble until reduced by half, adding any juices from the meat.

Stir in the capers and crème fraîche and simmer for a minute or two until the sauce is the desired consistency. Season generously with salt and pepper to taste. Remove and discard the garlic and herbs.

Spoon the sauce onto four warm plates and place the veal chops on top. Serve immediately, with some country bread on the side for mopping up the delicious sauce.

Sirloin steak with piquant tomato dressing

Serves 6

olive oil, for cooking
6 sirloin steaks, 200–250g each
sea salt and black pepper
few knobs of butter

Piquant tomato dressing
6 medium tomatoes
5 tbsp Tomato ketchup (see page 114)
2 tbsp Worcestershire sauce
1–2 tbsp Dijon (or wholegrain) mustard
few dashes of Tabasco
juice of 1 lemon
2 tbsp balsamic vinegar
2 tbsp olive oil
2 large shallots, peeled and chopped
handful of tarragon, leaves chopped
handful of parsley, leaves chopped

First, make the dressing. Halve the tomatoes, squeeze out the seeds, then finely chop the flesh and place in a bowl. Add the rest of the ingredients, except the herbs, and season with salt and pepper to taste. Set aside.

Heat a frying pan with a little olive oil until hot. Season the steaks with salt and pepper. Sear them in the hot pan in batches for 1–1½ minutes on each side, depending on thickness. Add a few knobs of butter to the pan during cooking and spoon the melted butter over the steaks to baste them. When ready, they will feel springy if lightly pressed.

Transfer the steaks to a warm plate, lightly cover with foil and leave to rest in a warm place for about 5–10 minutes. Meanwhile, stir the chopped tarragon and parsley into the dressing.

Slice the steaks thickly on the diagonal, arrange on warm plates and spoon over the dressing. Serve with Chunky chips (see page 206) and a side salad.

Fillet of beef with tomato &
tarragon dressing

Serves 6

1.2kg prime beef fillet (in one piece,
   cut from the thick end)
sea salt and black pepper
2 tbsp olive oil
few handfuls of wild rocket leaves

Tomato and tarragon dressing
500g (about 6) ripe plum tomatoes
5 tbsp Tomato ketchup (see page 114)
2 tsp Worcestershire sauce
2 tsp Dijon mustard
dash of Tabasco
juice of ½ lemon
2 tbsp balsamic vinegar
2 tbsp extra virgin olive oil
2 shallots, peeled and finely chopped
large handful each of tarragon and flat
   leaf parsley, chopped

To make the dressing, cut each tomato in half and squeeze out the seeds. Finely chop the flesh and place in a large bowl. Add the rest of the ingredients except for the herbs, and mix well. Season well with salt and pepper to taste. Cover with cling film and chill for at least 20 minutes or until ready to serve.

Heat the oven to 200°C/Gas 6 and put a roasting pan inside to heat up. Trim any fat or sinew from the fillet of beef and season all over with salt and pepper. Heat a non-stick frying pan with a little olive oil over a high heat. When it is very hot, add the beef and sear for 1½–2 minutes on each side until evenly browned all over. Lightly oil the hot roasting pan.

Transfer the beef to the roasting pan and place in the oven. Roast for 25 minutes for medium rare beef – it should feel a little springy when lightly pressed. Transfer the fillet to a warm platter and leave to rest for 10 minutes.

Serve the beef warm or at room temperature. Slice it thickly and arrange the slices overlapping on a serving platter. Pile the rocket into the centre. Stir the chopped herbs into the tomato and tarragon dressing and spoon over the beef. Accompany with new potatoes if you like.

Pot-roasted beef with root vegetables

Serves 4

1.2kg beef sirloin
2–3 tbsp plain flour
sea salt and black pepper
2 large carrots, peeled and halved
  lengthways
1 swede, peeled
1 large kohlrabi, peeled
2 large leeks, trimmed
4 tbsp olive oil
1 head of garlic, halved horizontally
150ml red wine
300ml Beef stock (see page 249)
handful of thyme sprigs
handful of rosemary sprigs
1 tsp black peppercorns
1 tsp coriander seeds

Heat the oven to 180°C/Gas 4. Trim off any excess fat and sinew from the beef. Mix the flour with a generous pinch each of salt and pepper on a wide plate. Roll the beef in the seasoned flour to coat, shaking or patting off any excess. Set aside.

Cut all the vegetables into large chunks. Put a large cast-iron casserole or heavy-based pan over a medium-high heat. Add a thin layer of olive oil and tip in the carrots, swede and a little seasoning. Fry for 4–5 minutes, stirring frequently, until golden brown. With a slotted spoon, transfer to a colander set over a large bowl to drain off any oil. Next, fry the kohlrabi, leeks and garlic, with a little more oil if necessary. Add to the colander.

Sear the beef in the hot pan, adding a little more oil if necessary, for 8–9 minutes until evenly browned all over. Transfer to a plate and set aside. Pour the red wine into the pan, stirring to deglaze, and let bubble until reduced by two-thirds. Stir in the stock. Return the beef and any juices released to the pan.

Spoon the vegetables around the beef and add the herbs, peppercorns and coriander seeds. Cover with a lid and transfer to the oven. Cook for about 25–30 minutes for medium-rare beef. Transfer the beef to a platter, cover with foil and leave to rest in a warm place for about 15 minutes.

Just before carving, spoon the vegetables onto a serving platter and keep warm. The sauce will be quite thin; to thicken it if required, boil to reduce slightly, then pass through a fine sieve into a warm jug. Thinly slice the beef and add to the platter. Serve with some rustic bread and a side salad if you wish.

Spicy beef curry

Serves 8–10

2kg good-quality lean braising beef or
 chuck steak
sea salt and black pepper
4 tsp garam masala
4 tbsp natural yoghurt
4–5 tbsp light olive oil
4 large sweet onions, peeled and finely
 chopped
4 garlic cloves, peeled and finely
 chopped
5cm knob of fresh root ginger, peeled
 and finely grated
4 tbsp tomato purée
2 tbsp caster sugar, or to taste
2 x 400g cans chopped tomatoes
800ml Beef stock (see page 249)
small handful of coriander, leaves
 separated, stalks finely chopped
6–8 cardamom pods
15–20 curry leaves
6 long green chillies

Spice mix
4 tsp coriander seeds
4 tsp cumin seeds
1 tsp fennel seeds
1 tsp fenugreek seeds (optional)
4 tsp mild curry powder
1 tsp ground turmeric

Cut the beef into bite-sized chunks, put into a bowl and season with salt and pepper. Sprinkle with the garam masala, add the yoghurt and toss to coat. Cover with cling film and leave to marinate in the fridge for at least 30 minutes, or overnight. Remove and set aside before you start to prepare the curry.

For the spice mix, toast the coriander, cumin, fennel, and fenugreek if using, in a dry pan, tossing over a high heat for a few minutes until the seeds are fragrant. Tip into a mortar, add a pinch of salt and grind to a fine powder. Stir in the curry powder and turmeric.

Heat a thin film of olive oil in a large cast-iron casserole or a heavy-based pan. Add the onions, garlic, ginger and a little salt and pepper. Stir, then cover and cook for 8–10 minutes until the onions are soft, lifting the lid to give the mixture a stir a few times.

Add a little more oil, tip in the ground spice mix and cook, stirring, for 2 minutes. Add the tomato purée and sugar and stir over a medium-high heat for a few minutes until the onions are lightly caramelised. Add the tomatoes, beef stock, coriander stalks, cardamom pods, curry leaves and whole green chillies.

Add the beef and stir until well coated in the sauce, then partially cover the pan with a lid. Simmer very gently, stirring occasionally for 3–4 hours, depending on the cut of beef, until the meat is meltingly tender.

To serve, ladle the curry into warm bowls and scatter over the coriander leaves. Accompany with a steaming bowl of basmati rice or warmed Indian bread.

Beef rib-eye with baby turnips in port

Serves 4

5 tbsp olive oil
400g baby turnips, washed and trimmed
few thyme sprigs
sea salt and black pepper
1 tsp Chinese five-spice powder
few knobs of butter
200ml port
1 tsp soft brown sugar
4 boneless rib-eye of beef steaks, about
    250g each and 3cm thick, trimmed

Heat 3 tbsp olive oil in a heavy-based pan and add the turnips, thyme and seasoning. Sauté for a minute, then add the five-spice and a couple of knobs of butter. Cook, tossing occasionally, for 8–10 minutes until golden brown.

Pour in the port, standing well back as it may flambé. Sprinkle in the sugar, stirring to dissolve, then let bubble for about 5 minutes until the liquor is reduced and syrupy.

Season the beef and sear in a hot ovenproof pan with the remaining oil. Fry for 3–4 minutes on each side, adding a knob of butter to finish off the cooking. For medium rare beef, the meat should be slightly springy when pressed. Rest the steaks in a warm place for 5 minutes before serving, with the glazed turnips.

Roast rump of lamb with herb couscous

Serves 6–8

6–8 rumps of lamb, about 200g each
few rosemary sprigs
4–5 garlic cloves, halved but not peeled
1 tbsp black peppercorns
olive oil, to drizzle
sea salt and black pepper

Herb couscous

350g couscous
600ml lamb or chicken stock
2–3 tbsp Vinaigrette (see page 250)
large handful of parsley, leaves chopped
large handful of mint, leaves chopped
handful of coriander, leaves chopped

Lightly score the fat of the lamb in a criss-cross pattern. Place in a large dish and scatter over the rosemary, garlic and peppercorns. Drizzle all over with olive oil and season with pepper. Cover with cling film and leave to marinate in the fridge for at least 2 hours, preferably overnight.

Heat the oven to 200°C/Gas 6. Heat a large ovenproof pan on the hob. Remove the lamb rumps from the marinade, drain and brown them in the hot pan in two or three batches for 2–3 minutes on each side. Return all the lamb to the pan and put into the oven for about 8–10 minutes to finish cooking. The rumps should feel slightly springy when pressed. Cover the lamb loosely with foil and set aside to rest in a warm place for 10–15 minutes before serving.

Prepare the couscous while the lamb is cooking. Bring the stock to the boil. Put the couscous into a large bowl and pour over the boiling stock. Cover the bowl with cling film and leave to soak for 10–15 minutes. Fluff up the couscous grains with a fork, drizzle over the vinaigrette and season with salt and pepper to taste. Reserving a little for garnish, add the chopped herbs and fork through.

Slice the lamb thickly on the diagonal. Pile the herb couscous onto warm plates and arrange the lamb on top. Sprinkle with the remaining herbs and serve.

Roast lamb with paprika & oranges

Serves 6–8

1 part-boned leg of lamb, about 2.4kg,
  with knuckle bone left in
1 tsp sweet paprika
1 tsp smoked paprika
1 tsp ground ginger
sea salt and black pepper
little drizzle of olive oil
4–5 garlic cloves, halved with skins left on
2 oranges, sliced

Heat the oven to 220°C/Gas 7. Trim away any excess fat from the lamb, then lightly score the surface fat in a criss-cross pattern. Mix the sweet and smoked paprika with the ground ginger and a pinch each of salt and pepper. Rub all over the lamb, including the boned-out cavity, with a little olive oil. Place the lamb on a rack over a large roasting pan and stuff the boned cavity with the garlic cloves and half of the orange slices. Pour a splash of water into the pan.

Roast the lamb in the oven for 20 minutes, then reduce the oven setting to 190°C/Gas 5 and roast for a further 20 minutes per 500g for pink lamb. If during roasting the top appears to be darkening too quickly, cover with foil. About 30 minutes before you calculate the lamb will be ready, lay the remaining orange slices over the meat.

Transfer the lamb to a warm platter, cover loosely with foil and leave to rest in a warm place for 10 minutes. Carve the lamb into slices and serve with new potatoes and a salad.

Honey mustard pork chops

Serves 6–8

6–8 pork chops, about 200g each
olive oil, to brush

Marinade
2 tbsp Dijon mustard
4 tbsp wholegrain mustard
6 tbsp runny honey
4 tbsp Worcestershire sauce
4 tbsp light soy sauce

Mix the marinade ingredients together in shallow bowl. Add the pork chops and turn to coat well. Cover with cling film and leave to marinate in the fridge for a few hours or overnight.

Heat a griddle pan or barbecue (or grill) until hot. Scrape the excess marinade off the chops and save it. Brush the chops with a little olive oil. Griddle, barbecue or grill for 4–5 minutes on each side or until cooked through, basting with the marinade from time to time. Leave the chops to rest in a warm spot for 5–10 minutes.

Serve the pork chops accompanied by a side salad and crusty bread.

Pressed belly of pork

Serves 6–8

1.3kg pork belly, ideally in one piece
sea salt and black pepper
olive oil, to drizzle
2 heads of garlic (unpeeled), halved
    horizontally
handful of thyme sprigs
splash of white wine
450ml Chicken stock (see page 248)

Caramelised apples

20g unsalted butter
3–4 Braeburn apples, cored, peeled and
    cut into wedges
50g caster sugar
1 spring onion, trimmed and finely sliced
few tarragon sprigs, leaves chopped

Heat the oven to 170°C/Gas 3. Season the pork flesh with salt and pepper, then turn the pork belly over and score the skin with a sharp knife. Rub all over with olive oil, salt and pepper.

Place the garlic, halved side up, on a lightly oiled roasting tray and scatter over the thyme sprigs. Lay the pork belly on top, fat side up. Trickle with a little more olive oil and sprinkle with a little more sea salt. Add a splash of white wine, cover the tray with foil and bake for 1½ hours. Remove the foil, baste the pork with the juices and return to the oven, uncovered, for another ½–1 hour until tender. Continue to baste the pork occasionally with the pan juices.

Transfer the pork to a clean roasting tray to cool. Place another tray on top and weigh down with a tin or weights to flatten the pork. Allow to cool and leave for several hours or overnight in the refrigerator to set the shape.

To make a gravy, skim off the excess fat from the roasting tray, then place on the hob over a medium heat. Deglaze with the chicken stock, scraping the bottom of the tray to release any sediment. Boil steadily until reduced and thickened.

Heat the oven to the highest setting, probably 240°C/Gas 9. Cut the pressed pork into individual portions or squares and pat the skin dry with kitchen paper. Place the pork squares, fat side up, in a roasting tray and drizzle with olive oil and a generous pinch of sea salt. Roast for 15 minutes until the skin is golden brown and crisp. Trim the sides of the pork pieces to neaten after roasting if you like.

For the apples, melt the butter in a wide non-stick frying pan. Dredge the apples in the sugar and add to the pan when the butter begins to foam. Fry for 3–4 minutes on each side over a medium heat until caramelised. Toss in the spring onion and tarragon.

Rest the pork for 5 minutes, then serve with the gravy, warm caramelised apple wedges and vegetables of your choice.

Glazed gammon with pineapple salsa

Serves 6

1 unsmoked boned gammon joint, about
   2.6kg, soaked overnight

1 large carrot, peeled and cut into
   3 chunks

1 large onion, peeled and halved

2 large celery sticks, cut into 3 chunks

1 bay leaf

few thyme sprigs

1 tsp black peppercorns

about 30–40 cloves

little oil, to oil

3 tbsp marmalade

3cm knob of fresh root ginger, peeled
   and finely grated

2 tbsp light soy sauce

2–3 tbsp water

Pineapple salsa

1 large ripe pineapple

1 small cucumber

1 red chilli, finely chopped

handful of coriander, leaves only,
   chopped

handful of mint, leaves only, chopped

sea salt and black pepper

1 tbsp sesame oil

2 tbsp olive oil

few dashes of Tabasco sauce

juice of ½ lemon

Drain the gammon and place in a large cooking pot. Cover with fresh water, bring to the boil and allow to bubble gently for 5–10 minutes. Skim off the scum and froth that rise to the surface, then pour off the water and re-cover the joint with fresh cold water. Bring to the boil, skim, then turn the heat down to a simmer and add the vegetables, herbs and peppercorns. Simmer for about 2 hours, checking the liquid from time to time and topping it up with hot water as necessary.

Lift the gammon out of the pot onto a chopping board and leave to cool slightly. (If the liquor is not too salty, save it to make a pea and ham soup.) While still warm, cut away and discard the skin and most of the fat, leaving an even layer. Score lightly in a criss-cross pattern, then stud a clove in the middle of each scored diamond.

Heat the oven to 190°C/Gas 5. Place the gammon in a lightly oiled roasting pan. Mix together the marmalade, ginger, soy sauce and water to make a glaze and brush all over the gammon to coat evenly. Roast for 20–25 minutes, basting several times, until browned and nicely glazed. You may need to turn the pan around halfway through to ensure that the joint colours evenly.

Make the salsa in the meantime. Cut away the peel and 'eyes' from the pineapple, then slice and remove the core. Cut the slices into 1cm cubes and place in a large bowl. Peel the cucumber, halve lengthways and scoop out the seeds, then finely dice the flesh. Add to the pineapple with all the other ingredients and mix well. Let stand for at least 20 minutes.

Rest the cooked gammon, covered with foil, in a warm place for 15 minutes. Carve into thin slices and serve with the pineapple salsa and vegetables of your choice.

Roast charlotte potatoes with chorizo

Serves 4–6

1kg medium Charlotte potatoes,
  scrubbed
sea salt and black pepper
olive oil, to cook
200g fresh (or smoked) chorizo sausage,
  chopped into bite-sized pieces
chopped parsley, to sprinkle

Heat the oven to 200°C/Gas 6. Boil the potatoes in salted water for 7–9 minutes. Drain and peel when cool enough to handle, then cut in half.

Heat a thin layer of olive oil in an ovenproof frying pan, add the chorizo and fry until it starts to release oil. Toss in the potatoes, season well, then roast in the oven for 15–20 minutes until golden brown. Sprinkle with chopped parsley. Delicious with simple chicken and fish dishes.

4 ways with potatoes

Chunky chips

Serves 4

1kg potatoes (eg Desirée or King Edward),
  scrubbed or peeled
sea salt and black pepper
5 garlic cloves (unpeeled)
few thyme sprigs
few rosemary sprigs, leaves only
olive oil, to drizzle

Heat the oven to 220°C/Gas 7 and place a sturdy roasting tray inside to heat up. Cut the potatoes into 1cm thick chips. Par-boil in a pan of salted water for about 5–7 minutes until just tender when pierced with a skewer. Drain well and pat dry with a tea towel.

Tip the potatoes onto the hot roasting tray and scatter over the garlic and herbs. Drizzle generously with olive oil and sprinkle with salt and pepper. Toss the potatoes to coat, using a pair of tongs.

Bake in the oven for 10–15 minutes until the chips are golden brown and crisp, turning them a few times. Drain on kitchen paper and serve immediately.

Champ with spring onions & broad beans

Serves 4–6

1.5kg floury potatoes (eg King Edward),
    peeled and halved or quartered if large
sea salt and black pepper
50g butter, plus an extra knob to serve
450ml milk
150ml double cream
5–6 spring onions, trimmed and
    finely chopped
400g skinned broad beans or peas
handful of chives, chopped

Boil the potatoes in salted water for 12–15 minutes until tender, then drain thoroughly. Mash the potatoes while still hot, then stir through the butter.

Bring the milk and cream to the boil in another pan. Add the spring onions and broad beans or peas and cook for 2 minutes until the beans are tender. With a slotted spoon, transfer the onions and beans to the potatoes, then gradually stir in enough of the creamy milk to achieve a good texture. Season well.

Reheat the champ, stir through the chopped chives and top with the knob of butter to serve. Perfect with rustic stews, braised meat dishes or as part of a hearty brunch.

Sautéed potatoes with paprika

Serves 4–6

1kg Charlotte or other waxy potatoes,
    scrubbed
sea salt and black pepper
olive oil, to cook and drizzle
mild paprika, to sprinkle

Boil the potatoes in salted water for 7–9 minutes. Drain and peel while still hot (wearing rubber gloves). Cut the potatoes into 1cm cubes and drizzle with a little olive oil. Spread out on a tray, season well and leave to cool.

Heat a little olive oil in a wide frying pan over a medium-high heat. Add the diced potatoes and cook, turning occasionally, until golden brown, crisp at the edges and tender. Drain on kitchen paper. Serve warm, sprinkled with mild paprika and sea salt. Lovely with fish or poultry dishes.

desserts

Berry crumble
Serves 4

**600g mixed berries (blueberries,
blackberries, raspberries etc.)**
1 orange
8 large mint leaves, shredded
1–2 tbsp caster sugar, to taste

Crumble
60g plain flour
25g chilled unsalted butter, diced
30g demerara sugar
30g rolled oats

To serve
natural yoghurt

Heat the oven to 190°C/Gas 5. For the crumble, put the flour and diced butter in a bowl and rub together with your fingertips to a crumbly texture. Stir in the demerara sugar and rolled oats. Spread out on a large baking tray and bake for 15 minutes or until golden brown and crisp, giving it a stir halfway through.

Divide the mixed berries among individual ovenproof dishes. Grate a little orange zest over each dish, then halve the orange and squeeze a little juice over the berries. Scatter the shredded mint over the berries along with the caster sugar to taste. Top with a layer of crumble.

Bake for 10–12 minutes, just to warm through. Serve warm, with a dollop of yoghurt.

Macerated summer berries

Serves 4

200g strawberries, hulled and
   quartered if large
450g other mixed berries
   (eg raspberries, redcurrants and
   blackberries)
2 tbsp icing sugar
150ml Muscat (or other sweet dessert
   wine)
clotted cream, to serve

Toss all of the berries together in a bowl with the
icing sugar and Muscat. Cover and leave to macerate in the fridge for
15–20 minutes.

Divide the berries among individual bowls, spoon
over the liquor and serve with a dollop of clotted cream.

Cherries with almonds & mint

Serves 4

500g ripe cherries, pitted
1–2 tbsp caster sugar
splash of amaretto liqueur
squeeze of lemon juice
50g flaked almonds, toasted
small handful of mint leaves, chopped
clotted cream or crème fraîche, to serve

Warm the cherries and sugar in a non-stick pan until the sugar begins to dissolve and the cherries start to release their juices. Add the amaretto and lemon juice and cook for a few more minutes until the liquid has reduced down.

Divide the cherries among small serving bowls and scatter over the toasted almonds and chopped mint.

Serve topped with a generous dollop of clotted cream or crème fraîche.

Blueberry & redcurrant eton mess

Serves 6–8

300g redcurrants, plus sprigs to finish
300g blueberries
2 tbsp caster sugar, plus extra to coat
4 tbsp kirsch (optional)
600ml double cream
2 tbsp icing sugar

Meringue nests
2 large egg whites
pinch of salt
100g caster sugar

For the meringue nests, heat the oven to 100°C/ Gas ¼. Using a hand-held electric beater, whisk the egg whites in a clean, grease-free bowl with the pinch of salt until they hold firm peaks. Gradually whisk in the sugar, 1 tbsp at a time. Continue to whisk until the meringue is glossy and holds its shape.

Spoon or pipe the meringue into round discs, about 2cm thick, on a lined baking tray. Bake for at least 2 hours until slightly crusty on top, then turn off the heat and let the meringues dry out in the oven for 6 hours or overnight. Peel the meringues off the baking parchment and store in an airtight container for up to a week.

Put half the fruit into a dry non-stick pan with the sugar and kirsch, if using. Cook over a high heat for 1½–2 minutes until the berries soften and begin to bleed. Crush lightly with a fork and push the fruit through a non-reactive sieve into a large bowl. Leave to cool completely.

Whip the cream together with the icing sugar in another bowl until it forms soft peaks. Crush 2 meringue nests and fold them through the cream with the remaining berries. Fold or ripple through the cooled berry coulis.

Spoon the mixture into a large glass bowl or onto individual serving plates. Coat the remaining redcurrants with a little caster sugar and use to decorate each plate.

Caramelised banana split

Serves 4

4 ripe bananas
8 tbsp caster sugar
2–3 scoops each of different ice creams
    (eg vanilla, chocolate, strawberry)
150ml double cream, lightly whipped
sweetened desiccated coconut, to
    sprinkle (optional)
4 glacé (or pitted fresh) cherries

Chocolate sauce
100g dark chocolate, broken into pieces
2 tbsp runny honey
75ml double cream

Peel the bananas and cut in half lengthways. Place cut side up on a sturdy baking tray and sprinkle evenly with the sugar. If you have a cook's blowtorch, wave it over the bananas until the sugar has caramelised. (Otherwise, preheat the grill to its highest setting and flash the bananas under the grill until golden brown and bubbling). Leave to cool until the sugar has firmed up.

Make the chocolate sauce in the meantime. Put all the ingredients in a bowl set over a pan of simmering water and stir occasionally until the chocolate has melted and the sauce is smooth. Take the bowl off the pan and leave to cool.

Arrange two banana halves on clear serving dishes (ideally oval or oblong), with the caramelised sides facing outwards. Place a scoop of each flavoured ice cream between the banana halves. Drizzle with chocolate sauce, then spoon or pipe over the whipped cream. Sprinkle with the coconut, if using, and top each banana split with a cherry. Serve immediately.

Baked ricotta with caramelised peaches

Serves 4

25g butter, plus extra (softened),
   to grease
85g icing sugar, plus 2 tbsp to dust
500g ricotta cheese, drained
2 large eggs
finely grated zest and juice of 1 lemon
4 ripe peaches, stoned and cut into
   wedges
3–4 tbsp caster sugar, to dredge

Heat the oven to 200°C/Gas 6. Generously butter the base and sides of four ramekins, then dust with icing sugar, tilting the ramekins from side to side to ensure an even coating.

Mix the ricotta, eggs, lemon zest and icing sugar in a large bowl with a fork until evenly combined. Spoon into the ramekins and stand on a baking sheet. Bake for 15–20 minutes until golden brown around the edges and quite firm in the middle. Leave to cool.

Dredge the peach wedges in caster sugar. Fry in a non-stick frying pan with the remaining butter until caramelised. Add the lemon juice, shaking the pan to deglaze. Take off the heat.

Turn out the ricottas onto individual plates. Arrange the caramelised peaches around and spoon over any pan juices to serve.

Iced berries with white chocolate sauce

Serves 4

125g blueberries
125g raspberries
125g blackberries
125g redcurrants
125g strawberries, hulled and quartered
200g white chocolate

Arrange the fruit in a shallow freezer container or on a baking tray and freeze for at least 2 hours or overnight until solid.

Break the chocolate into small pieces and place in a bowl set over a pan of barely simmering water, making sure the bowl isn't in direct contact with the water. Allow the chocolate to melt slowly, stirring occasionally, until smooth. Pour the melted chocolate into a warm small serving jug. If not serving immediately, keep the chocolate sauce warm by sitting the jug in a pan of hot water.

Divide the frozen berries among four chilled plates. Drizzle the warm chocolate sauce over the fruit at the table.

Spiced apple cake

Serves 8

1kg cooking apples (about 5 or 6)
50g caster sugar
30g butter, plus extra to grease
2 ripe Braeburn or Cox's apples
juice of 1 lemon
225g wholemeal flour
1½ tsp baking powder
½ tsp bicarbonate of soda
¼ tsp fine sea salt
175g soft brown sugar
1 tsp ground cinnamon
1 tsp ground ginger
½ tsp freshly grated nutmeg
½ tsp ground cloves
1 large egg, lightly beaten
50ml light olive oil
2 tbsp apricot jam, to glaze
1–2 tbsp water

Peel, core and slice the cooking apples. Place

in a wide pan with the sugar and butter. Cook over a high heat for 10–15 minutes until the apples have broken down to a pulp and any excess water has cooked off. Transfer to a bowl and cool completely. You should have about 475g purée.

Heat the oven to 170°C/Gas 3. Line and lightly grease

a 23cm cake tin with a removable base. Peel, core and finely slice the eating apple, using a mandolin or sharp knife. Place in a bowl and pour over most of the lemon juice and a splash of water; set aside.

In a large bowl, mix together the wholemeal flour,

baking powder, bicarbonate of soda, salt, sugar and ground spices. Make a well in the centre and add the egg, olive oil and apple purée. Fold into the dry ingredients until just combined.

Transfer the mixture to the prepared cake tin and

gently level the top with a spatula. Bake the cake for 30 minutes until it feels just firm to the touch in the centre. Working quickly, overlap the sliced apples in concentric circles on top, leaving a margin around the edge. Brush the slices with a little lemon juice and return to the oven for a further 30–35 minutes until a skewer inserted into the centre comes out clean.

Let the cake cool slightly before unmoulding onto a

wire rack. Warm the apricot jam with the water, stirring until smooth. Brush over the top of the cake to glaze. Serve warm.

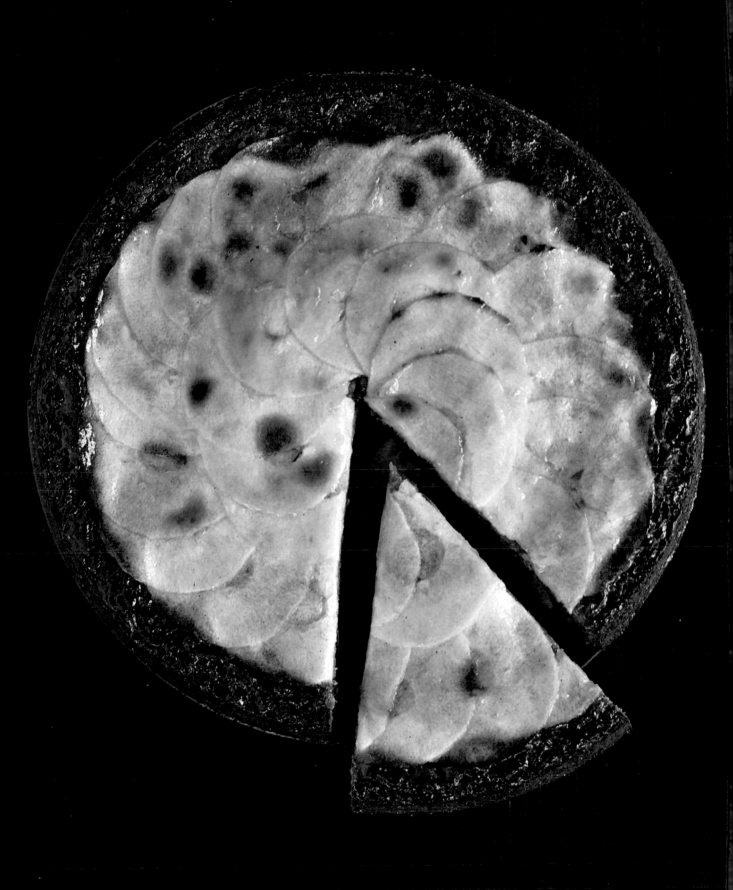

Pavlova with roasted rhubarb fool

Serves 6

1½ tsp cornflour, plus 1 tsp extra to dust
150g caster sugar
3 large egg whites (ideally from eggs
    about 1 week old)
1 tsp vanilla extract
½ tsp white wine vinegar
icing sugar, to dust
mint sprigs, to finish

Roasted rhubarb fool

500g rhubarb, trimmed and roughly
    chopped
a little butter, to grease
3–4 tbsp caster sugar
a little honey, to drizzle
400ml Greek yoghurt

Heat the oven to 140°C/Gas 1. Draw 6 circles, 8cm in diameter, on a sheet of silicone paper or baking parchment. Invert the paper onto a lightly oiled baking sheet and lightly dust with cornflour. Mix the cornflour with 1 tbsp of the sugar in a small bowl and set aside.

Beat the egg whites in a clean, grease-free bowl to firm peaks, taking care not to overwhisk. Gradually beat in the remaining sugar, 1 tbsp at a time, and whisk until thick and glossy. Fold through the cornflour mixture, vanilla and vinegar.

Spoon the meringue into a large piping bag fitted with a 1–1.5cm plain nozzle. Pipe concentric rounds over each circle to create a disc, then pipe two rings on the rim to form a shell. Bake for 40–45 minutes until dry and crisp. Turn off the oven and leave the meringues to cool slowly inside. (Ideally make them the evening before and leave to cool in the oven overnight.) Peel the meringues off the paper and store in an airtight container.

For the rhubarb, heat the oven to 200°C/Gas 6. Place the rhubarb in a lightly buttered roasting tin, sprinkle with the sugar and toss well. Roast for 15–20 minutes until tender. Tip the rhubarb and juices into a bowl, drizzle with honey and leave to cool completely.

To serve, ripple the roasted rhubarb and juices through the yoghurt to make a fool. Dust the meringue shells with a little icing sugar and place one on each serving plate. Spoon in the rhubarb fool and top with a mint sprig.

Gordon's trifle

Serves 4–6

Custard

400ml milk
120ml double cream
1 vanilla pod, split
6 egg yolks
60g caster sugar
1 tbsp cornflour

Trifle

2 tbsp muscovado sugar
4 peaches, stoned and sliced into
    wedges
few knobs of unsalted butter
4–5 tbsp Grand Marnier, or to taste
1 large jam-filled Swiss roll, cut
    into 1cm slices

Topping

2 x 200g tubs of crème fraîche
1 tbsp muscovado sugar
1 vanilla pod, split
oil, to oil
2 tbsp caster sugar
100g salted peanuts (or unsalted
    if you prefer)

To make the custard, put the milk and cream into a heavy-based saucepan with the seeds from the vanilla pod. Heat gently to infuse. In a large bowl, whisk together the egg yolks, sugar and cornflour. When the cream begins to bubble up the sides of the pan, take off the heat and slowly pour onto the eggs, whisking all the time. Pour through a fine sieve back into the hot pan. Return to a medium-low heat and keep whisking until the custard thickens. Set aside to cool.

For the trifle, scatter the muscovado sugar in a wide non-stick pan and melt over a medium heat, swirling it around as it begins to caramelise. Add the peaches, toss to mix and allow to take on a little colour before adding a few knobs of butter. Sprinkle with 2 tbsp Grand Marnier and let bubble until the liqueur has reduced right down and the fruit is tender, but retaining its shape. Leave to cool.

Line the bottom of a large serving bowl with the Swiss roll slices and drizzle with 2–3 tbsp Grand Marnier. Spoon the caramelised fruit on top, followed by the custard. Cover the bowl with cling film and chill for least 2 hours, or preferably overnight.

For the topping, mix the crème fraîche with the muscovado sugar. Add the seeds from the vanilla pod and stir until evenly combined. Spread on top of the trifle and refrigerate.

For the peanut brittle, have ready a lightly oiled baking sheet. Toss the caster sugar and peanuts in a dry non-stick pan over a high heat to caramelise the sugar and toast the peanuts. When the caramel turns golden brown, tip the mixture onto the baking sheet in a single layer. Leave to cool and set, then crush roughly in a large bowl with the end of a rolling pin.

Just before serving, scatter the peanut brittle evenly over the top of the trifle.

Berry & champagne soup

Serves 4

125g blackberries
125g blueberries
125g redcurrants
125g raspberries
handful of mint leaves
2–3 tbsp caster sugar
200ml natural yogurt
200ml double cream
300ml Champagne or sparkling wine,
   chilled

Tip all the berries into a blender and whiz to a purée. Add the mint leaves and sugar to taste, and blitz until the mint is finely chopped. Pour in the yogurt, cream and Champagne and whiz until evenly blended and frothy.

Pour the soup into serving glasses or individual bowls and serve immediately.

Helen's eve's pudding

Serves 4–6

Sweet pastry
150g butter, softened to room
  temperature
100g caster sugar
4 egg yolks, beaten
300g plain flour, plus extra to dust
pinch of salt

Filling
4 Granny Smith apples
2 tbsp caster sugar
1 tbsp water

Meringue topping
2 egg whites
4 tbsp caster sugar
few drops of vanilla extract

To make the pastry,
cream together the butter and sugar, using a hand-held electric mixer until pale and creamy. Gradually add the egg yolks, then incorporate the flour and salt until the mixture is evenly blended and crumbly, adding 1–2 tbsp cold water if it seems too dry. Bring the dough together with your hand, press into a ball, flatten slightly and wrap in cling film. Chill for at least 30 minutes.

Roll out the pastry
thinly on a lightly floured surface and use to line a 20cm tart tin with removable base. Line the pastry with baking parchment or foil and fill with baking beans. Refrigerate for at least 20 minutes.

Make the filling
in the meantime. Peel, core and chop the apples and place in a pan with the sugar and water. Cook gently for about 10 minutes until the apples are soft but still holding their shape. Tip onto a plate and leave to cool completely.

Heat the oven
to 180°C/Gas 4. Bake the pastry case blind for 15 minutes until golden at the edges, then remove the foil and beans and bake for another 5 minutes or until the base is cooked. Set aside to cool. Increase the oven setting to 200°C/Gas 6.

For the meringue,
beat the egg whites, using a hand-held electric whisk until stiff. Gradually beat in the sugar, a spoonful at a time, with the vanilla until fully incorporated and the meringue is stiff.

Spread the apple
filling in the pastry case and top with the meringue. Peak the meringue with a fork to give it an attractive finish. Bake for 15–20 minutes until the meringue is golden brown. Cool slightly, then slice into individual portions and serve warm.

Summer berry & vodka jelly

Serves 5–6

200g caster sugar
500ml water
3 sheets leaf gelatine
60ml vodka
200g raspberries
200g blueberries
400g strawberries, hulled and
    quartered
handful of basil leaves

Dissolve the sugar in the water in a pan over low heat. Meanwhile, soak the gelatine in cold water to soften. Bring the sugar syrup to the boil and let boil for a few minutes. Take off the heat, squeeze the gelatine leaves to remove excess water, then add to the sugar syrup, stirring to dissolve. Leave to cool, then mix in the vodka.

Mix the raspberries, blueberries and strawberries in a bowl. Shred the basil leaves and toss with the berries, then divide among 5–6 small serving glasses. Pour over just enough of the cooled vodka syrup to cover the berries. Chill for a few hours until set.

Yoghurt sorbet

Serves 6–8

350ml water
225g caster sugar
3 tbsp liquid glucose
300ml natural yoghurt
100ml fromage frais

Pour the water into a heavy-based pan, add the sugar and liquid glucose and place over a low heat. Stir occasionally until the sugar has dissolved, then increase the heat and boil for 3–4 minutes. Remove from the heat and cool completely.

Beat the yoghurt and fromage frais together in a bowl until smooth and creamy. Mix in the cooled syrup.

Pour the mixture into an ice-cream machine and churn until almost firm, then scoop the sorbet into a suitable container and freeze for several hours until firm. If you do not have an ice-cream machine, freeze the mixture in a shallow container and beat with a fork several times during freezing.

Delicious served with both hot and cold desserts, or scooped into glasses with fresh fruit.

party time

Crab wraps with mango salsa

Serves 6

300g white crabmeat
½ red chilli, deseeded and very finely
    diced
1 shallot, peeled and very finely diced
small handful of coriander, leaves
    chopped
1 tbsp wholegrain mustard
6–7 tbsp Mayonnaise (see page 250)
sea salt and black pepper
squeeze of lime juice
1 large head of Iceberg lettuce, washed

Salsa
1 red chilli, deseeded and very finely
    diced
1 small red onion, peeled and very finely
    diced
juice of 1 lime
1 tbsp sesame oil
1 tbsp olive oil
2 large ripe mangoes, peeled and cubed
handful of mint leaves, shredded

Put the crabmeat into a bowl and run your fingers through the meat to pick out any little bits of shell. Add the chilli, shallot and coriander and fork through to mix. Stir the mustard into the mayonnaise, then mix enough into the crabmeat to bind the mixture. Season with salt and pepper and add lime juice to taste.

For the salsa, combine all the ingredients except the mangoes and mint in a bowl. Season lightly with salt and pepper.

Separate the lettuce into leaves, then trim the sides to give 10–12cm wide strips. Carefully flatten the trimmed lettuce leaves on a chopping board, without tearing them. Place a heaped tablespoonful of crab filling along one end of each strip and roll the lettuce leaf around the filling to encase it. Place, seam side down, on a plate. Continue until you've used all the crab filling.

When ready to serve, stir the chopped mangoes and shredded mint into the salsa and spoon into a serving dish. Arrange the crab wraps on a platter and sprinkle with salt and pepper. Serve immediately.

Mixed fish sashimi

Serves 4–6 as a starter

400g sashimi-grade swordfish fillet

400g sashimi-grade centre-cut tuna fillet

300g sashimi-grade skinless salmon fillet

1 very fresh mackerel, about 300g, filleted (optional), or use an extra 100g each swordfish, tuna and salmon

To serve

light soy sauce

pickled ginger

wasabi paste

Trim off any dark flesh from the swordfish and neaten the edges (you can save all the fish trimmings to make fishcakes). Trim the tuna to a neat log and neaten the edges of the salmon fillet. Carefully check over the salmon and mackerel fillets for pin-bones, removing any you find with kitchen tweezers.

Wrap each fish in cling film and place in the freezer for 45 minutes to allow the flesh to firm up slightly, making them easier to slice neatly.

Take the fish from the freezer and remove the cling film. Thinly slice each fish with a very sharp knife and overlap the fish slices in neat rows on a serving platter. The sashimi can now be chilled for a few hours until ready to serve. Bring to the table with little dipping bowls of light soy sauce, pickled ginger and wasabi paste.

Crispy parma ham with asparagus

Serves 10

30 asparagus spears, trimmed
sea salt and black pepper
15 slices Parma ham
3–4 tbsp olive oil

Blanch the asparagus in boiling salted water for 2–3 minutes until bright green and just tender. Drain and refresh under cold running water, then drain again and pat dry.

Cut each Parma ham slice in half lengthways and wrap around an asparagus spear.

Fry the asparagus rolls in a hot pan with a little olive oil, turning frequently, for 2–3 minutes until the ham is crisp. Grind over a little pepper and serve.

Cherry tomato & feta kebabs

Serves 10

300g feta cheese
30 cherry tomatoes
30 small basil leaves
extra virgin olive oil, to drizzle
black pepper

Cut the feta into 2cm cubes and halve the cherry tomatoes. Thread them onto cocktail sticks, sandwiching a feta cube between two tomato halves. Thread a basil leaf onto each end and arrange the kebabs on a serving plate.

Just before serving, drizzle a little extra virgin olive oil over the kebabs and sprinkle with a little freshly ground pepper.

Parma ham, sage & parmesan puffs

Makes about 35

85g unsalted butter, plus extra
   to grease
220ml water
100g plain flour
pinch of salt
3 medium eggs, beaten
100g Parma ham, finely chopped
4–5 sage leaves, finely shredded
40g Parmesan, finely grated

Heat the oven to 200°C/Gas 6. Put the butter and water in a heavy-based saucepan. Heat slowly to melt the butter, then turn up the heat and bring to a rolling boil. Meanwhile, sift the flour with the salt. As the liquid comes to the boil, tip in all the flour and take off the heat. Beat vigorously with a wooden spoon until the mixture forms a paste and leaves the sides of the pan. Leave to cool.

Beat the eggs into the paste, a little at a time, until shiny and smooth. The mixture should have a dropping consistency (you may not need all of the egg). Beat in the Parma ham, sage and Parmesan until evenly incorporated. Lightly grease a large baking sheet.

Spoon the mixture into a piping bag fitted with a 1.5cm plain nozzle and pipe into 3–4cm rounds on the baking sheet, spacing well apart. Bake for 20–25 minutes or until risen and golden.

Stuffed courgette rolls

Serves 6–8

4 small courgettes, trimmed
olive oil, to oil and drizzle
sea salt and black pepper
250g ricotta
juice of ½ lemon
splash of extra virgin olive oil
handful of basil leaves, chopped
50g pine nuts, toasted
balsamic vinegar, to drizzle

Slice the courgettes lengthways, using a swivel vegetable peeler or a mandolin and select about 40 good strips. Place the courgette strips on an oiled tray and brush with olive oil. Season with salt and pepper and chill for 20 minutes.

Mix the ricotta with the lemon juice, extra virgin olive oil and seasoning to taste, then fold in the chopped basil and pine nuts. Place a small teaspoonful of ricotta mixture on one end of a courgette strip and roll up. Repeat to use up all the filling.

Arrange the courgette cannelloni on a plate and grind over some black pepper. Drizzle with a little olive oil and balsamic vinegar and serve.

Manchego & membrillo on olive bread

Serves 4

4 thin slices of olive bread
150g manchego cheese
8 tsp membrillo paste
extra virgin olive oil, to drizzle
sea salt and black pepper

Cut each slice of bread into four. Cut the manchego cheese into medium slices and remove any outer rind.

Place a slice of cheese on each bread slice and top with a spoonful of membrillo paste. (If using firm membrillo, cut into thin slices and place on top of the cheese.)

Drizzle with a little olive oil and sprinkle with sea salt and a grinding of black pepper. Arrange the tapas on a serving platter.

Minty mojito

Serves 10

plenty of crushed ice
150g caster sugar
6–8 limes, halved
1 large bunch of mint
250ml white or light rum
about 500ml soda water

Half-fill a large jug with crushed ice and sprinkle
in the sugar. Grate the zest from one of the limes into the jug, then
squeeze the juice from all of the limes and add to the jug. Drop in the
spent lime halves that haven't been zested.

Snip the leaves from the bunch of mint into the jug and
gently crush against the ice with a spoon.

Pour in the rum and add soda water to taste. Stir well
and pour into chilled glasses to serve.

Blueberry & pomegranate fizz

Serves 10

150g blueberries
2 tsp caster sugar
1 pomegranate
1 bottle of Champagne, well chilled

Heat a frying pan until hot, then tip in the blueberries and sugar and add a little splash of water. Place over a medium heat for a minute to slightly soften the berries. Tip onto a plate and leave to cool. Meanwhile, carefully prise out the seeds from the pomegranate avoiding the bitter membrane.

Put a spoonful of blueberries and a sprinkling of pomegranate seeds into 10 champagne flutes. Pour over the chilled Champagne and serve at once.

basics

Chicken stock

Makes about 1.5 litres

2 tbsp olive oil
1 carrot, peeled and chopped
1 onion, peeled and chopped
2 celery sticks, chopped
1 leek, washed and sliced
1 bay leaf
1 thyme sprig
3 garlic cloves, peeled
2 tbsp tomato purée
2 tbsp plain flour
1kg raw chicken bones
sea salt and black pepper

Heat the olive oil in a large stockpot and add the vegetables, herbs and garlic. Cook over a medium heat, stirring occasionally, until the vegetables are golden. Stir in the tomato purée and flour and cook for another minute. Add the chicken bones, then pour in enough cold water to cover. Season lightly. Bring to the boil and skim off any scum that rises to the surface. Reduce the heat and leave to simmer gently for 1 hour.

Let the stock stand for a few minutes (to cool slightly and allow the ingredients to settle) before passing through a fine sieve. Leave to cool. Refrigerate and use within 5 days, or freeze the stock in convenient portions for up to 3 months.

Fish stock

Makes about 1 litre

2 tbsp olive oil
1 small onion, peeled and chopped
½ celery stick, sliced
1 small fennel bulb, chopped
sea salt and black pepper
1kg white fish bones and trimmings
    (or crab or lobster shells)
75ml dry white wine

Heat the olive oil in a stockpot and add the onion, celery, fennel and a little salt and pepper. Stir over a medium heat for 3–4 minutes until the vegetables begin to soften but not brown. Add the fish bones and trimmings with the wine, then pour in enough cold water to cover the ingredients. Simmer for 20 minutes, then remove the pan from the heat and leave to cool.

Ladle the stock through a fine sieve and discard the solids. Refrigerate and use within 2 days, or freeze in smaller quantities for up to 3 months.

Vegetable stock

Makes about 1.5 litres

3 onions, peeled and roughly chopped
1 leek, washed and roughly chopped
2 celery sticks, roughly chopped
6 carrots, peeled and roughly chopped
1 head of garlic, halved crossways
1 tsp white peppercorns
1 bay leaf
few thyme, basil, tarragon, coriander
    and parsley sprigs, tied together
200ml dry white wine
sea salt and black pepper

Put the vegetables, garlic, peppercorns and bay leaf in a large stockpot and pour on cold water to cover, about 2 litres. Bring to the boil, lower the heat to a simmer and leave to cook gently for 20 minutes. Remove the pan from the heat and add the bundle of herbs, white wine and a little seasoning. Give the stock a stir and leave to cool completely.

If you have time, chill the stock overnight before straining. Pass the liquid through a fine sieve. Refrigerate and use within 5 days, or freeze in smaller amounts for up to 3 months.

Beef stock

Makes about 1.5 litres

1.5 kg beef or veal marrow bones,
    chopped into 5–6cm pieces
2 tbsp olive oil, plus extra to drizzle
2 onions, peeled
2 carrots, peeled
2 celery sticks, peeled
1 large fennel bulb, trimmed
1 tbsp tomato purée
100g button mushrooms
1 bay leaf
1 thyme sprig
1 tsp black peppercorns

Heat the oven to 220°C/Gas 7. Put the bones in a roasting tray and drizzle with a little olive oil. Roast for about 1 hour, turning over halfway, until evenly browned. Meanwhile, cut the onions, carrots, celery and fennel into 5cm chunks.

Heat the olive oil in a large stockpot and add the vegetables. Cook, stirring frequently, over a high heat until golden brown. Stir in the tomato purée and cook for another 2 minutes. Add the browned bones and pour in enough water (about 2–2.5 litres) to cover them and the vegetables. Bring to a simmer and skim off the froth and scum that rise to the surface. Add the mushrooms, bay leaf, thyme and peppercorns. Simmer for 6–8 hours until the stock has a deep, rich flavour.

Leave to stand for a few minutes, then pass the stock through a fine sieve. Leave to cool, then refrigerate and use within 5 days, or freeze in smaller portions for up to 3 months.

Mayonnaise
Makes about 300ml

2 large egg yolks
1 tsp white wine vinegar
1 tsp English or Dijon mustard
sea salt and white pepper
300ml groundnut oil

Put the egg yolks, wine vinegar, mustard and a pinch of salt in a food processor (fitted with a small bowl attachment, if you have one). Whiz for a few minutes until thick and creamy. With the motor running, slowly trickle in the groundnut oil in a thin stream until the mayonnaise is thick and emulsified. Season generously with salt and pepper. (If the mayonnaise splits as you are adding the oil, transfer the mixture to a jug. Put another egg yolk, a little mustard and seasoning into the food processor and whiz for a minute or two, then slowly add the split mayonnaise. It should re-emulsify.)

Transfer the mayonnaise to a bowl or jar, cover and refrigerate. Use within 3 days.

Vinaigrette
Makes about 250ml

100ml extra virgin olive oil
100ml groundnut oil
3 tbsp white wine vinegar
1 scant tsp Dijon mustard
sea salt and black pepper

Put the ingredients into a measuring jug and whisk together to emulsify (or use a stick blender to combine).

Pour into a clean squeezy bottle or screw-topped jar and seal. Keep in the fridge or cool larder for up to a week. Shake well before each use.

index

Project director Anne Furniss
Creative director Helen Lewis
Project editor Janet Illsley
Designer Katherine Cordwell
Editor Kathy Steer
Photographers Lisa Barber & Jill Mead
Food stylist Mark Sargeant
Home economist Emily Quah
Production Vincent Smith, Ruth Deary

First published in 2010 by
Quadrille Publishing Limited
Alhambra House, 27–31 Charing Cross Road, London WC2H 0LS
www.quadrille.co.uk

Text © 2010 Gordon Ramsay
Photography © 2006, 2007 Jill Mead & © 2008 Quadrille Publishing Limited
Design and layout © 2010 Quadrille Publishing Limited

The recipes in this compilation have been previously published in the following books from THE **f** WORD series: Sunday Lunch, Fast Food and Healthy Appetite.

Cataloguing in Publication Data: a catalogue record for this book is available from the British Library.

ISBN 978 184400 904 6

Printed in China

Picture Credits:
Photographs by Lisa Barber: 4; 6–7; 8; 13–28; 37; 42; 45–50; 55–60; 64; 66; 70; 75; 82–101; 109; 112; 117–121; 124–5; 126; 130; 137; 140; 142; 152; 162; 165; 166; 168; 171; 180; 183; 193–196; 200; 205–210; 221–222; 237

Photographs by Jill Mead: 10; 30; 32; 34; 35; 38–41; 43; 52; 53; 63; 68; 72; 76–81; 102–106; 110; 115; 122; 129; 133; 134; 139; 144–151; 155–160; 173–179; 184–190; 198; 202; 211–218; 225–234; 238–247